Dedication

To my wife Marilyn, who for 25 years prayed faithfully that her husband would experience the same grace, mercy, and power of the Lord Jesus that he regularly proclaimed to others.

Contents

Foreword

I cannot remember when I last read such a detailed and challenging autobiography as that of Dr. Harvey Brown. His professional career has been quite diverse—including being a U.S. Army Chaplain as well as a college administrator at Asbury College. Now as president of Impact Ministries, he is spreading the love and the fire of God through itinerant work. This book is his own testimony, revealing intimate details of how the power of God has impacted his own life and that of his family and friends. As a credible witness, Dr. Brown reveals God's profound answers to deep human need in response to the destructive power of secret sins—both our own as well as those committed against us.

Dr. Brown has clearly understood what I would agree is the heart of this current new move of God. This he has done through the lenses of his own powerful experiences and interactions. I quote, "It was clear to me now that Father was cleansing the bride, making her fit for the revelation of His Son the Groom. I needed to plainly declare the truth of God's power, not just to forgive and heal, but to keep us continually clean in the holiness, mercy, and grace of Father's love" (quoted from pages 88-89).

Harvey Brown has taken the time to recall the detail which helps us, as his readers, realize that this is not just someone else's story, but, yes, God can and will do the same in our lives as well. This book is not just light reading. Dr. Brown allows the reader to walk with him through the gut-wrenching cost and difficult choices that radical encounters with God inevitably lead one into. As a result, God is using him to help in the process of creating new wineskins for the new wine.

He reluctantly identifies with the blind man in John chapter 9 in the New Testament. While still reeling from the most profound and life-changing encounter with God in his entire life, he finds himself embroiled in a controversy not of his making. The heated debate wasn't really centered on the miracle, but on peripheral issues concerned with the impact of change on existing institutions, traditions and beliefs. But just as the blind man finds a new release in the worship of the Savior who comes to him, Harvey Brown's new freedom is focused on Jesus.

This book offers hope to those who are bound by secret sins of pornography and sexual addictions. It gives the reader a clear presentation of the cleansing power of the Good News of our Lord Jesus Christ and the power and life of the Spirit that God is offering to all, regardless of denominational affiliations. Anyone who hungers and thirsts after righteousness shall be filled.

Carol and I were delighted to have been used of the Lord, albeit in a small way, to see this man of God healed, set free and empowered to bring the healing love of God to this generation.

I heartily recommend this work to you.

John Arnott, Senior Pastor
Toronto Airport Christian Fellowship

Author's Preface

They overcame him by the blood of the Lamb and by the word of their testimony; they did not love their lives so much as to shrink from death (Revelation 12:11).

I know how good it feels to spend time with a new acquaintance and come away from the encounter sensing that I have really gotten to know that person—that he or she has been real and transparent with me; that I have been allowed into their interior space; that they haven't played it safe or close to the vest; that they have opened their hands and their heart for me to see who they really are. On the occasions when this has happened I have felt trusted and fulfilled because we have moved beyond superficiality and social custom. We have entered each other's world.

I hope that you feel the same way after reading this book. I am going to risk myself with you and allow you entry into my interior world. I am going to tell you the truth—the good, the bad, and the ugly. Sometimes it will be painful for me, but I am determined to be transparent to the best of my ability.

This book is a true story of renewal. It is the story of how I, as a professional Christian, began a quest for God that led me into a head-on encounter with Him who is a consuming fire. You will discover how I was changed through the fire—and how these changes affected my family as well as my ministry. You will discover that there can be real gaps between a believer's profession of faith and the victory (or lack thereof) that they experience. And you will encounter a Father love that is full of mercy for needy souls. It's a story of great contrasts, much like that contrast between my new office and the old one.

I really love my new office. It's flooded with light because three exterior walls are filled with windows. I can look outside and watch the birds as they perch in the fir tree just a few feet away. Or I can gaze across the street and observe young college students leaving their dormitory and hurrying off to class. The transparency of the glass allows me to see out…and just as easily allows others to see in.

This is quite a change from my last office, which was located on an interior hallway in the administration building at Asbury College. It had no windows, so I filled the walls with memorabilia and the trappings of accomplishment. If you stood in the hallway and looked in the direction of my desk, I would have been invisible because of the barriers presented by the walls and their hangings. Even if you entered the office and looked at the stuff on the walls, you still would not have known me—you would have only known about me.

One of my goals in this book is to tear down any walls that obscure, and strip away the trappings of accomplishment behind which I have hidden, so that I might become transparent and let you see who I really am…and the powerful miracle of grace and renewal that God has worked in my life. By the time you get to the end (if you hang in there that long) you may be able to say with me "God has indeed done a notable miracle." Or you may go so far as to identify with my experiences and find yourself hoping, because of my miracle, for a similar miracle in your own life. Whatever the case, I pray that once you have read these pages you will see, at least from my perspective, a dimension of God's grace that has caused me to fall head-over-heels in love with my Savior…when I recognized that He was head-over-heels in love with me.

All of the persons and events described in this book are real. Some names and circumstances have been altered to conceal the identity of the characters, but the essence of the situations described is accurate. I obtained the express permission of many of the persons who appear here to tell their stories in hope that Jesus would receive great glory through the miracles He has done in their lives.

I am grateful to everyone at Revival Press (a division of Destiny Image), and especially staff publisher Elizabeth C. Allen, for their professionalism, encouragement, and persistence in getting this book to press. And of course, I want to thank my family: my wife Marilyn and children Chip, Candace, Elizabeth, and Harrison. They have loved me even when I have been unlovely. They have suffered with me when my behavior has been insufferable. They have walked with me through the fire. And they have celebrated with me as we entered the dance of God. Come join us in our recently ignited passion for holiness and renewal.

To Him who is able to keep you from falling and to present you before His glorious presence without fault and with great joy—to the only God our Savior be glory, majesty, power and authority, through Jesus Christ our Lord, before all ages, now and forevermore! Amen (Jude 24-25).

memorize

1

An Ordinary Miracle

No eye has seen, no ear has heard, no mind has conceived what God has prepared for those who love him (1 Corinthians 2:9).

I could see deep anguish in Reneé's eyes. My presence in her office was the result of a message I had found in my voice mail—one that asked for prayers to be lifted up for Reneé's husband, Bud. I was not fully prepared for the news she had to share.

I knew Reneé Jenness because my job as a college administrator frequently brought me through her office. Like many college or seminary staff members in our town, Reneé was helping to put her husband through school (at nearby Asbury Theological Seminary).

Lately Bud had been having digestive problems. Physician tests revealed the presence of a mass in his colon.

I adjusted my chair so that I could speak privately with Reneé. "Tell me what's going on. What are the doctors saying?"

"I'm so scared," replied Reneé hesitantly. "Bud's been sick off and on, and we haven't been able to get anything concrete. And now the alarming results of these tests...."

"You're really scared, aren't you?"

"I'm terrified! Bud's father died of cancer. His older brother already had a colostomy because of Crohn's Disease. It's like this stuff"—she waved her hand in the air—"is running through his family. And now...now it's him."

"Reneé," I asked, "do you think that Bud would like me to pray with him, and anoint him for healing?"

My mind was running a hundred miles an hour as my heart reached out to Reneé. Bud needed a miracle, and I sensed that he needed it now. People around campus already were praying in response to this widely circulated voice-mail request, but I felt like I needed to be praying personally for Bud—anointing him with oil and praying in faith for his healing.

"Yes," she sighed, "I really think that he'd want you to do that."

Reneé agreed to call Bud and see if he could come to my office the next day after his classes were finished. We shared a brief prayer, asking God to begin a miracle process in Bud's life. Then I gently squeezed her hand as if to say that Father had everything under control.

As I left her office, I was aware of the presence of the Holy Spirit. *Thank you, Father, for your grace*, I thought. *Manifest your glory through these things, in Jesus' name.*

These things all seemed so natural to me now. It was November 1996, and less than a week before...during Halloween...I had been preaching in Salem, Massachusetts, and had witnessed Father manifesting Himself in healings, salvations, and deliverance. If the Holy Spirit was released through saints' prayers to work so powerfully in a city where darkness reigned, how much more could He be released in a city where God's Word was honored and the Spirit's power proclaimed from both church pulpit and classroom lectern?

The phone rang shortly after I returned to my desk. It was Reneé. "How about three o'clock tomorrow?" she asked.

"Looks good," I replied. I penciled the phrase "Bud Jenness—healing" into my Day-Timer for Friday, 3 p.m. I simply had this feeling....

The next day was the standard Friday routine for a college administrator: an early-morning coordination meeting, a chapel service at 10 a.m., a luncheon appointment with a faculty member, and then phone calls to return. Yet within each activity I felt an underlying current of prayerfulness running just below the surface. I found myself almost groaning in inward prayer—intercession—for the ministry to Bud that would come in the afternoon.

I did not then, nor do I now, see myself as a healer. But I had become convinced that it is Father's heart to heal His children. Through the operation of the gifts of the Spirit, which include healings and miracles, Father uses the Church to bless those who need His touch. I was beginning to see recurring instances of Father's miraculous intervention on behalf of His needy children, and this intervention was beginning to flow through me as I became open to the Holy Spirit's active presence in my life. God's miraculous interventions were becoming regular occurrences. I was finally getting to do the things described in the Book.

Through my study of Acts 19, I had become aware that Luke differentiated between two different kinds of divine intervention: miracles and extraordinary miracles. There were times when God chose to act outside of direct human agency or touch, and these "extraordinary miracles" were accomplished beyond the mechanism of direct human contact. For examples, consider the healings and deliverance resulting from the distribution of Paul's sweatrags (handkerchiefs) and aprons (Acts 19:11-12), as well as the people healed by contacting Peter's shadow (Acts 5:15).

Yet the scriptural record clearly suggests that God most often works through people—through "ordinary" miracles—to accomplish His will. These healings and activities of divine intervention are accomplished by the Holy Spirit's power operating through human tools. God chooses to use the weakness of human flesh so that the glory of his divine majesty might be revealed. The human touch would, in the mystery of His sovereign plan, convey the divine touch as well.

This is why I felt it so important to touch Bud when I prayed for him, and not just offer prayers from a distance. Through recent experience, my faith had been boosted to a new level. Not only could

I conceptualize healing, but I had seen it done. I had already been used by God in this way. I was fully prepared for Father to continue in the present moment the work that was accomplished by the stripes laid on His Son's back.

By the time my secretary announced that Bud and Reneé were in the outer office, I had been made confident that this prayer appointment would be a clear visitation of God's manifest presence.

After introducing myself to Bud, I invited the couple to sit for a while so we could talk before prayer. This was important, if Bud were to feel comfortable praying and would be relaxed in the flow of the Holy Spirit.

As we shared, I could see in Bud's face and hear in his voice that he feared something was terribly wrong with the genetic structure of men in his family. Now, at his young age, the specter of death was peering over his shoulder and glaring frightfully into his life. Reneé's face reflected the same apprehension.

I shared with them the powerful healings that I had seen over those past three weeks, and we reviewed some promises from Scripture concerning healing, healing prayer, and anointing. With each word, I felt an increasing compassion—what I believed Father was feeling—for this young couple.

"Bud, I believe with all my heart that Father wants to heal you. With your permission and agreement, I want to pray for you, anoint you with oil, and believe for you a healing directly from Father's hand."

As we stood facing each other in a small circle, I carefully opened a little vial of perfumed anointing oil that I had retrieved from my pocket. Moistening my finger with the glistening liquid, I carefully traced the pattern of a cross on Bud's forehead. A sweet and pungent odor filled the office. I began to groan quietly in my spirit.

"Father, oh Father," I prayed, "You know everything about us. You know how we are made. You were with us when we were formed in the secret place of our mother's womb. And You know everything about my brother Bud."

Tears began to form under my eyelids, and as I blinked the droplets puddled and then ran down my cheeks. The Lord's compassion was rising up and beginning to overwhelm me.

I began to pray the Word. " 'For I know the plans I have for you,' declares the Lord, 'plans to prosper you and not to harm you, plans to give you hope and a future.' "

Bud took a deep, halting breath.

"And I speak life to you, Bud, and not death. I take authority, in the name of Jesus, over this mass in your colon. I curse it, in the name of Jesus, and I **command** it to leave. You, O Lord, have given me this authority, and I exercise it not in my strength but in the strength and power of the name that is above all other names, the name of Jesus. And I ask one other thing, Father. Let the doctors and all who attend to Bud know conclusively that You, and You alone, have done a mighty miracle in his body. Get great glory because of Your great love and power, in Jesus' name."

There was a feeling like fire in my hands as they rested on his head. I knew that something very important was happening —we were being visited by the manifest presence of the God of the universe. His holiness filled the room. Faith filled my heart. "Bud, I believe that when you get 'scoped' on Monday, the cancerous mass will be completely gone. I look forward to hearing a good report."

We embraced before they left. "Father is with you, Bud," I said. "I believe you are going to see His glory."

I thought of Bud and Reneé as the weekend progressed, and prayed that God would remove any anxiety they might be feeling while waiting for Monday's medical tests.

Late Monday afternoon, I received a call from Reneé, her voice giddy with excitement.

"You'll never believe what happened!" she gushed. But I had a feeling that I would.

"They prepped Bud for the test and inserted the scope. The doctor looked puzzled as the test progressed. He kept manipulating the scope through Bud's colon, looking for the mass. But there was nothing! Absolutely nothing!"

Reneé began to sob as she spoke. "The mass was gone! Praise the Lord! It was **completely** gone!"

We rejoiced together and praised Father over the phone.

"Bud is a new man," Reneé told me. "He said that he felt like he just received a reprieve from a death sentence and has been given his life back again."

For a moment I pondered her words. Indeed, I believed that he had.

2

A Stirring in the Nest

God's words are underneath everything. And if you listen carefully, you will hear them. (Ken Gire)

June 1994. I closed the magazine and placed it on the credenza. *How unusual*, I thought, *people laughing in church and falling on the floor.*

I had never sensed much hilarity in worship. Occasionally I heard folks chuckle or even laugh heartily at a sermon joke, but what *Christianity Today* described about a Vineyard Church in Toronto was quite far from my experience. I never expected to see that sort of thing in my lifetime, especially not in the circles that I traveled.

But there was no more time to ponder such things. Our family was preparing to move from Germany to Fort Jackson, South Carolina, where I would become Senior Pastor of the Main Post Chapel.

Being a U.S. Army chaplain was (most of the time) a great adventure. Our family had lived on three continents, traveled throughout Europe and Central America, and made friends around the world. As a young chaplain, I had been to Airborne School and served for seven years in infantry units caring for soldiers and their families. During the time we were stationed in the Republic of Panama, I was the "Jungle Expert" chaplain at the

Army's Jungle Operations Training Center (the school of jungle warfare) and also provided chaplain coverage for the Special Forces Group. I loved my soldiers and relished the challenge of relating the gospel to these young Americans who served their country so proudly.

In many ways, I had become a traveling evangelist, with a passion to see my troops get to know the Lord Jesus. And the kind of assignments I received from the Army provided real opportunity to see that happen.

When assigned to the Infantry Training Brigade at Fort Benning, I was in preaching heaven. Twice each Sunday morning I faced an overcrowded chapel packed with young clean-shaven recruits at some stage of their thirteen-week Initial Entry Training. Most Sundays there were soldiers sitting on the floor between the front pews and the chancel rail. I often had to push the pulpit furniture back against the wall so we could fill the chancel area with worshipers. "Just leave me an eight-foot circle to work in," I told them. "I hope that heaven's this crowded too!"

The different infantry training companies that comprised my congregation were scheduled in overlapping cycles, so every thirteen weeks I faced a congregation that was completely different. It also meant that, over a two-year period, I'd be proclaiming the Good News to over 20,000 different men. Hungry hearts were open hearts, and over 2000 men boldly professed faith in Christ during this period.

But the gospel's work wasn't limited to the hearts of trainees only: My preaching also affected career soldiers. One Sunday, when giving an invitation to accept Christ, I saw the First Sergeant from Alpha Company stand among his soldiers and pray the sinner's prayer. Another time, I led the Bravo Company commander—a Mormon—to true faith in Jesus Christ. These were exciting days of high adventure, and I couldn't imagine doing anything else.

Following my four-year tour in Central America, we returned stateside to begin what would be a five-year stint at Fort Monmouth,

New Jersey, the home of the Army Chaplaincy. After six months of mid-career "charm school," I was selected to remain on the staff and faculty of the Army Chaplain School and given responsibility for managing the design of a new chaplain-training model.

During this time, others began to recognize the preaching gift with which the Lord had entrusted me. I was invited more often to speak in our daily chapel programs and represent the chaplaincy at community and church events. Then came the call from the Commandant's secretary: "Chaplain Clanton wants to see you."

Chaplain Charles Clanton was a Southern Baptist who had risen to the rank of colonel and the position of Commandant of the Army Chaplain School. He was highly respected, and many chaplains considered him the leading candidate for the next Chief of Chaplains—and the rank of general. I knew him to be a deeply spiritual man with a marvelous ability to encourage those who worked for him. I had no idea why he wanted to see me: It was unusual to have a command performance with the "Old Man" (as soldiers called their commanders) without notice coming through the junior officer's immediate supervisor.

"Come on in, Harvey, and have a seat," smiled Chaplain Clanton when I was ushered into his office. I was directed toward a leather armchair next to a low table.

The dark walnut paneling lent an air of manly elegance and accomplishment to the office. Framed commendation certificates were intermingled with mementos of a long and distinguished military career. Charlie Clanton was what we called a "soldier's chaplain"—someone who loved and identified with his troops while selflessly serving them.

He left his desk and sat in a chair near me. "Harvey," Chaplain Clanton said, "I want to ask you a question. But I don't want you to answer immediately."

His words sounded like the beginning of a, "Boy, do we have a wonderful opportunity for you!" talk—which is Army lingo for,

"You're about to be transferred, soldier, and since you can't do anything to avoid it, just suck it up and drive on."

But I couldn't believe this would happen to me. I had been back from Panama for only two years, had been recently promoted, and was just beginning to hit stride in terms of my responsibilities and expertise in the "schoolhouse." I had even been brought up to the headquarters area by the Old Man to serve as his acting Executive Officer from time to time.

"Yes, sir," I replied. I hoped he couldn't see my heart beating through my uniform shirt.

"I've been watching you, Harvey. You've done a super job here at the school, and I appreciate it very much. But I sense that there's something else you'd rather be doing."

Oh no, I thought, *what could he possibly be thinking? I love the Chaplain School, the great coworkers, the prestige of being a young officer in such an assignment. There's no place I'd rather be.*

Chaplain Clanton continued. "I've heard you preach many times in our daily chapel services. You're a preacher, son, and a very good one at that. There's something that happens when you start proclaiming the Word that lets me know you're never happier than when talking about Jesus. Am I right?"

He certainly was. I loved my role at the school, but my passion was the proclamation of the gospel: I'd preach every chance I got. Most weekends, I was somewhere in New Jersey talking about Jesus. And my peers frequently asked me to take the preaching slot during daily chapel. "Yes, sir," I said. "I guess when the Lord called me to preach, He made me a preacher first, last, and always."

"Harvey, we need preachers in the Army. Not just counselors who are chaplains, not just good staff officers who wear the cross. We need preachers. And we need someone to model what good evangelical preaching can be right at the heart of the Chaplaincy. We need to show these new chaplains that good preaching matters."

I nodded, wondering where this was going.

"So I've talked to the Post Chaplain and Chief of Chaplains, and they've agreed that we need to transfer you..."

My mind began spinning wildly: *Why? Where? When?*

"...to the Post Chapel right here at Fort Monmouth. Next month you become the garrison chaplain and pastor of the home church of the U.S. Army Chaplaincy. Congratulations."

I sat there with a dazed expression on my face. In one month, I would become the model—the prototype—of a preaching chaplain for every new chaplain in the entire Army, as well as the pastor for a community of preachers from virtually every denomination represented in this country. I was staggered and yet exhilarated by the prospect.

Chaplain Clanton continued. "In my opinion, son, the Fort Monmouth Post Chapel is the most important pulpit in the Army. It should be the very best that we have, and I am committed to seeing that happen. Now I realize that as Commandant I am losing you as an asset. But at this point preaching is so critical for the Army that I'm willing to lose you from my staff so that your gifts can be better put to use. I have confidence, Harvey, that you'll be just what we need."

He paused, then added one other thing: "You know, very few people get to do what I've just done—I've just named my own pastor."

Indeed, he had.

* * * *

I gazed aimlessly out the window of the jetliner as we flew at 35,000 feet somewhere above the Atlantic. My mind drifted back to that conversation with Chaplain Clanton six years previously. Now I was once again going to be pastor of the home church for the Army chaplaincy, but in a different state. The orders bringing me from Europe to South Carolina assigned me to the Post Chapel, and the Army Chaplain School was moving from New Jersey to Fort Jackson.

My task once again would be to model evangelical pastoral ministry to the Chaplains Corps as Post Chapel pastor. I looked forward to it and also anticipated a great reunion with the Batlucks—friends and former parishioners.

Joe and Irene Batluck had been a part of my chapel family at Fort Monmouth. Joe had been the preaching "expert" at the Chaplain School, after finishing an additional masters degree in preaching at Princeton. He and Irene were key members of the chapel parish—she, the organist, and both of them junior-high youth leaders. Now they lived in Columbia, South Carolina, where Joe served as the Deputy Post Chaplain. They would again be part of my flock, and Joe would be my chaplain supervisor.

With no government housing available on the Fort, Marilyn and I purchased our first house not far from the post. After twenty-two years of parsonages and military housing, we were finally getting a taste of home ownership. We delighted in the new challenges of landscaping, placing azaleas, dogwoods, and redbuds throughout the clusters of tall pines surrounding the house. Our two older children were in college now, and there was a well-reputed high school located nearby where our two younger children would attend. Columbia looked like a place to settle for years to come. At least it seemed possible that I could stay at Fort Jackson long enough to reach retirement.

I had no idea how soon all that would change, based on a phone call from Joe Batluck half a year later.

One of Joe's responsibilities was to relate to chaplains on post about their assignments. He had called to let me know that he had talked earlier in the day with someone from the United States Army War College in Carlisle Barracks, Pennsylvania. They had been calling about me.

The War College is the Army's graduate school for strategic studies and the grooming place for future generals before they become brigade commanders. Assigned to the War College for one year, most officers graduate to the highest levels of leadership in the force. Why were they calling Fort Jackson to ask about me?

"Sounds like your name is up for assignment to Carlisle Barracks," Joe replied. "I know that the current Protestant pastor there is scheduled to leave in May."

My heart sank. Although the War College pulpit would be a platform for influencing the highest levels of Army leadership for years to come, why move now? We had been in our house only seven months, the kids loved their new high school, and I was starting to see results from the first stages of my ministry on post. It just didn't make sense.

I decided to call the Chief's office.

A chaplain wasn't normally supposed to call the Office of the Chief of Chaplains unless he had permission from his supervisor. Issues were to be resolved at the lowest possible level, and few things required a junior chaplain to talk directly with the Pentagon. But I decided I needed to contact the head of personnel, Chaplain Dennis Camp.

I had been friends with Chaplain Camp since my earliest days in the Republic of Panama. This soft-spoken Texan was one of my chaplain heroes—a man of immense integrity and moral courage. I had seen him take great personal and professional risk to stand up on behalf of a chaplain who had been treated unfairly by a commander. There was no one in the corps whom I respected any more than he.

I began by sharing with Dennis the phone conversation I had with Joe. "I'm not sure what to make of it," I finished. "Can you tell me anything from your end?"

There was a brief pause. "I'm really not free to talk in detail about it," said Chaplain Camp, "but I'll tell you this: If you haven't finished unpacking all your boxes from the Germany move, don't."

"Don't tell me I'm moving," I said. "I can't—just can't. We've bought our first house, the kids are in a new school. Things are starting to happen here in the congregation. To top things off, I'm not even high-enough rank to fill that slot."

"Look, Harvey, I know it's tough, but we need someone at the War College who can speak to these leaders week after week. I've been staffing this with the Deputy Chief. We both know you, and we both believe that you're the man for the job."

"But what about the rank thing?" I asked. "I know the promotion board just met and that I was considered for promotion to Lieutenant Colonel. But the results aren't going to be announced for another two or three months. Do you know something about the promotion list?"

"Nobody has seen the list, Harvey. Not even the Chief."

I became direct: Dennis' integrity and his love for me wouldn't allow him to lie. "So how can you even consider me for this job?"

He replied cautiously. "PERSCOM [Personnel Command] sends Pentagon assignment officers a list of those considered, but not selected, for promotion. Although we don't receive notice of those selected for promotion until the list is officially released, we know who hasn't been selected after the promotion board meets. And then we begin to project new assignments based on that information."

Now it made sense: Although he didn't officially know I'd be promoted, he had a list of those not promoted and I wasn't on it. I didn't have to be a rocket scientist to figure out that my name would be on the promotion list.

But now I'd have to relocate. My joy over an apparent promotion was trashed because of the forced move. And to top it all off, the relocation would be sudden. It was now March, and I might have to report to my new job before the end of May.

After I got off the phone with Chaplain Camp, I dialed Joe.

"You're right, brother," I said as soon as Joe came on the line. "I just finished talking to Dennis Camp, and he said my name was up for the War College pulpit, with a reporting date at the end of May!"

"Whew, that's incredible," said Joe.

"I don't know what to think."

"Look at the good side—and there are good sides," responded Joe. "You'll be promoted, Carlisle's a great post, and if you don't want the job, I'll take it! There's no other chaplaincy job I'd rather have."

We both chuckled for a moment, but I was still serious when I said, "Well, I'd give it to you if I could, Joe."

When I got home that night, I called a family meeting and unfolded the day's events as gently as I could—both the promotion and the imminent move. Everyone cried.

"Daddy, how could this happen?" one of the kids asked.

"The Lord's at work in our lives. And although right now I don't feel the least bit good about it, I'm in the Army. A soldier goes where he's sent, and I guess that means we're moving to Pennsylvania."

I didn't rest much that night. A feeling of accomplishment mingled with distress of sudden unsettledness. How could we absorb the costs of selling a house just months after purchasing it? I thought you needed to keep a house at least four years to break even. And how would the move affect the kids? Military kids had to go through so much anyway, without additional trauma like this.

I drifted off into a half-sleep, my mind filled with more questions than answers.

3

Stepping Out, Stepping Up

*Don't worry about what's ahead. In faith, go as far as you can.
From there, you can see farther.* (source unknown)

Secrets are sometimes heavy burdens to bear. For almost six weeks
I had been unable to discuss my situation beyond my smallest circle
of confidants—the Batlucks, my parents, and my immediate family.
No one was supposed to know about unreleased promotion lists; if
I were to announce to my congregation that I would be moving,
they'd think that word was leaked prematurely although no one
had yet seen the official results of the promotion board. I was keeping painfully quiet about the turmoil in my personal world.

I drew consolation from the close (albeit only once-a-month) fellowship with the ministerial association in Columbia. This gathering of about fifty of the city's clergy was a warm and congenial
assembly of men and women who opened their arms to me as a full
colleague, although my ministry environment was considerably different from theirs. Led by Brother Glenn Anderson, pastor of For-
est Drive Baptist Church, most represented either charismatic or
Pentecostal churches. There was a noticeable absence of mainline
denominations present.

One thing I appreciated about these people was the clear love and
respect they had for each other. Our monthly breakfast meetings

were full of prayer and deeply genuine fellowship. They had real interest in each other's ministries and took a real interest in me as well. In addition, the members planned ministry and outreach activities together, to win the community for Christ without selfish or parochial concerns about who would get the credit—or who would have the higher seat. Corporately, their heart's desire was to see Jesus glorified in South Carolina's capitol city.

It was a rainy winter Thursday morning when we gathered for our monthly meeting. Most of us had finished breakfast, and coffee mugs were being refilled. Glenn Anderson called for our attention.

"I received a call earlier this week from an old friend in Melbourne, Florida, and he told me something so astounding that I had to share it with you. But," he paused, "it was so incredible I didn't know if you'd believe it coming from a Baptist." After some laughter from us, Glenn continued. "I called the radio station down there and they sent me a transcript of what happened."

Glenn proceeded to read several pages of an account written by a Christian radio station manager in Melbourne, whose station experienced a spontaneous revival and powerful visitation of the Spirit of God. Randy Clark was a guest on a live call-in show when, by all accounts, the Holy Spirit began to manifest Himself in the station building and among the listening audience. We all sat in awed silence as Glenn recounted to us the amazing and rather strange occurrences.

Pastor of the St. Louis Vineyard Fellowship, Randy Clark had been the speaker at four days of meetings in Toronto, January 1994, when the "Toronto Blessing" began. Although I was vaguely familiar with these events (due to the magazine article I had read the previous year), I had nothing more than a passing interest in what was happening in Toronto or Melbourne. I was more worried about being back to the fort in time for my 10 a.m. counseling appointment. Watching the clock carefully, I knew that I should excuse myself in order to return to Fort Jackson on time.

But discussion was excited and animated, and the group decided to have Glenn pursue the possibility of Randy Clark speaking in Columbia. As I stood to go, several brothers waved good-bye. *They don't need my input,* I thought, *and I doubt that Fort Jackson folks would participate in a town event anyway.*

At the next meeting, during prayer, I revealed my upcoming move. I knew that the members' commitments to each other, as well as their distance from the fort, would prevent my disclosure from getting back to the base. My brothers and sisters gathered around me and prayed for God's mercy and grace to cover me and my family.

The rest of the meeting was spent discussing plans for the upcoming Randy Clark meetings. Clark had accepted Glenn's invitation to come to Columbia in May, and everyone was excited while planning the event. Again I excused myself from the meeting early, thinking that I would probably not be involved. My time and energies needed to be focused on moving, since there was so much to get ready.

As the date drew near for the promotion list's official release and the public announcement of my move, I found it harder to focus on tasks related to the chapel ministry. *There's not much use in pressing any issues right now or starting new programs,* I thought. *Let my successor handle that. He needs the freedom and flexibility not to be burdened with my stuff, but to begin whatever he feels best in doing.*

The jangling ring of my phone startled me out one of these daydreaming moments. "Call from the Pentagon for you," the secretary said. It was Chaplain Dennis Camp in Washington, and the sound of his voice told me something was wrong. "I'm really sorry to have to call you like this," he said.

"What do you mean, Dennis?"

"I just received the promotion list which is scheduled for release in 72 hours. I don't know what happened, but you're not on it."

I could feel the blood drain from my face. I eased myself back in the chair and closed my eyes trying to absorb the full impact of his words.

There was a long pause before Dennis spoke again. "It doesn't make sense to me. You weren't listed among the non-select early in the spring, so I could logically assume you were on the promotion list. But you're not. I tried to find out what happened, but no one knows: It's just like your name has fallen through the cracks."

I felt like it had. My family and I had been to hell and back trying to cope with the trauma of a sudden move, and now all of our preparation seemed to hit a brick wall. The shock was indescribable.

"So now what?" I said.

"I plan to leave you right where you are, Harvey. Just continue doing what you're doing...."

My mind drifted as Dennis kept talking. I grasped at any thought that could help me make sense of everything we had been through. Jerking the family around. Riding the roller coaster of emotions. Straining to get our act together for a sudden move. And now this one-hundred-eighty-degree turn-around.

Inside I was screaming, *Reverse engines. Bail out! Bail out!* I knew that in the next split-second something would happen that would change the course of my personal history.

"Dennis," I interrupted, "I'm going to retire."

* * * *

For several hours after hanging up the phone with Dennis Camp, I was talking almost non-stop with people who needed to know of my decision to retire.

Of course, I needed to notify my denomination. Since my United Methodist bishop reappointed me every year to the Army chaplaincy, I was responsible to notify his representative—my district superintendent in Virginia—about my decision to leave the military. He listened attentively, then asked if I was interested in "coming home" to serve a church in Virginia or Tennessee. I told him that I would consider it but that he should get back with me when he had something more concrete to discuss.

"There's one other thing that you should know," I added. "When I helped lead a retreat in Switzerland last year, Bishop Swenson from the Rocky Mountain Conference was a guest preacher. The bishop offered me an appointment to a Vail, Colorado, church if I were interested." I thought it a good idea to let him know that others were interested in me, since it could elevate my chances for a good appointment.

My next call was to our denomination headquarters in Nashville. Our Division of Chaplains and Related Ministries was the direct link between the United Methodist Church and the U.S. Army, and they needed to be informed of my decision. I was surprised when a director came on the line and asked me to apply for a job there. "Harvey, this might be the Lord's timing to bring you our way. Three of us are retiring over the next couple of years, and I'd like you to send your resumé right away. You'd love it here in Nashville."

It seemed tempting—I'd be relating to the Army but as an ecclesiastical official instead of a chaplain. To top it off, whenever I would visit a military installation, rules of protocol would demand that I be treated like a general officer. Commanders and chaplains would trot out their best dog-and-pony shows to impress me. And it would be sweet revenge to stay in general's guest quarters worldwide, especially considering that I was retiring early because I wasn't being promoted!

But I knew that I had no real interest in becoming a church bureaucrat and distancing myself from the aspects of ministry to which I felt most called. I realized that the offer wasn't for me and declined.

My next call—to Russell Williams, Director of Alumni Relations for Asbury College, my alma mater—started the events ultimately leading me into Christian higher education. I wasn't sure why, but I felt a need to call him, even if to only let him know that we might be moving. He suggested that I call the college vice-president and inquire about an opening in the administration.

Marilyn and I had a little game that we'd play together from time to time. She'd look at me and say, "What would you like to do when you grow up and quit playing soldier?" And I'd respond with whatever came to mind. Yet several times after playing this little game, we'd begin to talk seriously about what life would hold for us after I left the Army. And sometimes we had discussed how special it would be to return to Asbury College as part of the faculty or administration, since we were both alumni. This idea had been reinforced through contacts made during class reunions, as well as occasional and subtle encouragement from our former college president and mentor, Dr. Dennis F. Kinlaw. My call to Russell Williams reawakened this memory.

Following his advice, I immediately called Dr. David Lalka, whom I had met briefly the previous year but with whom I had never really had a conversation. I left a message for Dr. Lalka expressing interest in a possible college position, and he returned the call later that evening. By all indications, he was thrilled. An administration position had been open for some time, and although there were a number of qualified candidates, he did not consider any quite right for the job. The search had continued already two months beyond the deadline for filling the post.

According to Dr. Lalka, my profile and credentials were perfect—alumnus, donor, doctor, and parent. We made plans to meet the next day, when I went to pick up my daughter for the summer.

Little did I know as I finally stood on the threshold of Dr. Lalka's office at Asbury College that I was also standing on the threshold of a process that would lead me into the fire.

4

Like a Moth Drawn to Flame

Let us draw near to God with a sincere heart in full assurance of faith, having our hearts sprinkled to cleanse us from a guilty conscience and having our bodies washed with pure water (Hebrews 10:22).

From the moment I walked between stately white columns and stepped through the doorway of the Asbury College Administration building, I had a sense of divine destiny leading me back home. I loved this place because it was here—in the little village of Wilmore, Kentucky—that I had developed both the content and context for my Christian faith. I was returning to my roots, to my spiritual home.

I had transferred to Asbury in 1970 after completing almost four years at the University of Georgia. My time there was another story in itself.

My sister, two-and-a-half years older, was a student at the university, and as soon as I could drive I was making weekend pilgrimages to Athens. Sis would get me dates with girls from Athens High, and I would attend fraternity parties as the guest of guys who wanted to stay in her good graces. I was big stuff in my adolescent mind, far above the juvenile high-school scene: a collegian in waiting, just marking time in Macon until I could be a real Georgia Bulldog.

To fulfill my dream as soon as possible, I enrolled in the university one week after high school graduation. I got a head start on my college career by attending summer school. Also, because freshmen had to complete one full quarter before joining a fraternity, I'd be qualified for rush during the fall rather than having to wait until the winter. What could be better than attending Georgia football games with a coed on my arm and a fraternity pledge pin on my chest? Only becoming a BMOC—big man on campus.

It seemed that everything I thought I wanted or needed in order to be a "somebody" on campus came my way. Outwardly, everything looked great. I was president of my fraternity pledge class and elected an officer the day after I was initiated. I was "cool" because I worked in an exclusive men's store near campus. It was an extrovert's heaven: twenty-thousand students, and I was running with the best. Student government-appointed positions, my photograph plastered throughout the university yearbook, and the academic honors program were to come during the next three years.

But no matter how much recognition I achieved or how many goals I reached, inside I felt hopeless and worthless. I had terribly low self-esteem buried beneath my confident and cocky exterior. While on the outside I was Joe Cool, BMOC, Frat Man, on the inside I was a nobody—insecure and always looking for some way to emotionally prop myself up. Nothing seemed to satisfy the soul-deep emptiness I felt.

By my senior year, my collegiate dream had become a nightmare. My party was now a wake. I lived a life of spiritual and moral death where college was no longer a blast, even though I was more frequently "getting blasted." With my hedonism rushing me headlong towards hell, I sat in my apartment one night with my hands over my face.

Why not just end it all? I reasoned. Self-destructive thoughts were more common as my depression deepened. I was now recycling the idea of suicide. A litany of supposed successes paraded before me and, like the child declaring that the emperor had no clothes, mocked the emptiness of all the things I had considered so important.

Looking for fraternity brotherhood, I had instead found a drinking club. Arrogance—worn to cover my minimal self-esteem—so alienated me from my brothers that I eventually became an inactive member. *They're losers*, I had told myself, while really feeling deep in my heart that I was the true loser.

I had sought consolation in a relationship with JoAnn, one of the prettiest girls on campus, but like so many other things she was just a prop. I assumed that people seeing us together would respect me, but my dour outlook and self-absorption eventually pushed her away. I was still smarting over her break-up with me.

In my depression I had stopped attending classes, instead hanging out at the Student Center's Bulldog Room smoking, joking, playing bridge, and pretending to be the life of the party. During these times I was able to forget my internal feelings, if just for a little while. My grades had taken a nose dive. There I was, a zoology major in an international premedical honor society, about to make a D, F, and WF (Withdrew, Failing) in three five-hour major subjects.

No wonder suicide had become a recurring thought. Whenever I returned to my apartment and was alone, I had to confront the emptiness of my life. Everything that I thought would make me happy had failed to fulfill.

The box of barbiturates was still there in the drawer. *Wash the pills down with the rest of the whiskey in the bottle on the shelf, go to sleep, and say, "To hell with this world."* That seemed like the only alternative to the pain I felt in my soul. But I needed to do one other thing first.

If I were going to have one last shot at making an impression, I wanted to make sure that it was done right. Why not plan the funeral? My yearbook photo was great. I was the ultimate preppie in my bow tie and vested suit. I could see it in the Macon paper— obituary with photo, the list of honors and activities. Everyone would wonder why. The burden of achievement? The pressure of being so successful? But I would take the secret to my grave: I would kill myself because I was lost and lonely.

The plans for the funeral unfolded rapidly before me: Solid walnut casket, no tacky praying hands, a casket spray of white carnations (my fraternity flower). My fraternity brothers would be honorary pall bearers. In my mind's eye I could see the cortege winding its way up the paths of Rose Hill Cemetery. Believing that image was everything, I continued to ponder my grand exit.

But when I finished at last, sitting in an old overstuffed chair and feeling a macabre satisfaction over the details, a voice spoke to me. It uttered only three words. Whether the voice was heard by my ears or my mind, it hit me just the same:

"Who will mourn?"

"What do you mean, 'Who will mourn?' " I said aloud.

My mind raced to review those who would attend my funeral. My parents would mourn. My sister would mourn. But my fraternity would probably use the funeral as an excuse for an out-of-town party. Political figures would show up, but only because my dad was a lobbyist. The more I thought, the more I realized that my life had absolutely no impact beyond the immediate family circle. Here I was about to make my last big splash, but it looked to be more of a ripple.

My emotions ebbed even further. For so long I had worked to create an image, yet the final sculpture had been made of clay. It could not last. It would not last.

I finally came to a decision: There would be no suicide tonight. No, there must be some way to pull this thing together. Who could I talk with? Where could I find help?

Just two weeks before, my friend Toby and I had been on our way to play golf when two sharp-looking guys struck up a conversation with us in the parking lot. Since we had been in a hurry to leave, we chose to meet with them for dinner later that night.

Dave Wilcoxon and Ron Kyzer were not much older than we, but they certainly seemed to have their acts together. It turned out that they were staff members of Campus Crusade for Christ. As we were eating our meal, they had been sharing about Jesus. *Fanatics*, I remembered thinking.

After listening to what they had to say, I had still been convinced that my lifestyle and ethical decision-making process was exemplary. Those honors philosophy courses weren't lost on me. "Well, I understand your religious interest," I had said, "but I'm OK as I am. Everybody has the right to believe what they choose, and I'm just not where you guys end up. But I respect what you stand for."

I felt like I had dismissed their thesis with dispatch. The meal had been enjoyable, but I didn't need what they were offering. I had joined a church. I knew the Christmas and Easter stories. I believed that God existed. But all this talk of knowing Him in a real way made me a little uncomfortable.

As we had parted after dinner that night, Ron had smiled and waved. "Remember, guys, if you ever need to talk, I'm the last 'K' in the phone book."

Don't hold your breath, I had thought.

The ticking of the wind-up alarm clock counted off the sleepless moments of a never-ending night, and I grew even more despondent. Almost without thinking, I picked up the phonebook, turned to the right section, and found Ron Kyzer's name right where he had said it would be. You just couldn't get any more last than having a "y" and "z" in your name.

At 1:35 a.m. I dialed his phone number.

Ten minutes later Ron was knocking on my apartment door. When I let him in, he squeezed my shoulder and looked me in the eye. His presence let me know that he truly cared.

I blurted out all of my frustrations and dashed dreams. I described in detail and very colorful language my sense of hopelessness. Throughout everything, Ron listened carefully.

"Harvey, I'm not exactly sure how to respond. But do you mind if we pray together first?"

I nodded, feeling detached from anything he was saying.

After praying, Ron took out a small paper-backed Bible, turned a few pages, then underlined some words. He handed it to me so that I could read what he had underlined:

If we claim to be without sin, we deceive ourselves and the truth is not in us. If we confess our sins, He is faithful and just and will forgive our sins and purify us from all unrighteousness (1 John 1:8-9).

That was it! That was it! In an instant, I had illumination rather than human understanding. The moment I finished the last word I knew in my heart that the issue was sin—my sin! That's what had separated me from God. Even though I had given no intellectual assent to the concept of sin, sin nonetheless was controlling my life and killing me. But the Holy Spirit was leading me into all truth. He had shown me, through Ron's choice of scripture (1 John 1:8-9) that the remedy for sin was Jesus.

I felt like a cartoon character with a light bulb drawn above his head. I suddenly understood. I looked up at Ron. "What do I do?"

"Talk to God, just like I'm talking to you. He's not concerned with your words as much as He is the attitude of your heart. If you'd like, we can pray together—you take my words and make them your words. God will hear."

I began to pray phrase-by-phrase behind Ron. When I asked Jesus to come into my life, it was like my gut, which had been tied in knots for so long, was suddenly untied. I could literally feel the release. As I asked Him to forgive my sins, I felt as if someone had lifted a pack full of rocks from my shoulders. I knew—positively knew—that I belonged to Jesus and that my sins were forgiven. I was born again.

After I became a believer I sensed a call to ministry, although I really couldn't define what "ministry" meant. All I knew was that, from the first day of my new Christian life, all I wanted to do was talk about the Lord. Pursuing a medical career was no longer a passion, despite being a well-paid profession. No, I wasn't supposed to become a physician: The Lord had ministry in store for me.

Rather than waste my time and my parents' money, I withdrew from the university and spent the better part of a year trying to discover what the Lord had in store. I got my first clue at an all-night prayer meeting in Jim and Joy Shierling's house in Columbus, Georgia.

Dr. Tom Carruth, a professor at Asbury Theological Seminary, had sent Jim and Joy an audiocassette about a spontaneous revival that had broken out at a small Christian, liberal arts college in Kentucky. Classes were suspended for over a week as the Holy Spirit was poured out in continuous waves each day and night. We sat on the living room floor and wept as student after student, faculty members, and town people shared how the power of the Holy Spirit had touched them. They confessed sins to one another, prayed for one another, and sensed the cleansing and empowering work of God's presence in a special way. I had never heard of anything like that before, but I knew I had to go. The next day I quit my job, loaded my car, and drove to Kentucky.

I arrived just in time to watch the class of 1970 graduate. I slipped into one of the wooden seats in Hughes Auditorium and had the strangest sensation—that, just like sitting at the kitchen table in my childhood home, I was suddenly where I belonged. It felt right. It was right. Even before I enrolled, I knew that I was always going to be an Asburian.

When I transferred to Asbury College, I was like a dry sponge soaking up everything I could about my new faith. I learned the doctrines in class and chapel—the content of historic Christianity. And I learned the context of the faith—how to live it in relationships with friends and professors and other Christian men. The college's imprint was to be indelibly stamped on who I was and what I believed. My wife also bore this familiar mark. And my daughter as well.

Now, after twenty-five long years, I was standing on the steps of Asbury College, returning not as a student but as an administrator. Little did I know that I was returning to school because the Lord had much more to teach me—and that it would be through the fire.

5

Seeing Through a Glass Darkly

You cannot confess to God what you will not first admit to yourself.
(David Seamands)

No matter where I turned, God seemed to be just around every corner. The smallest details of the transition from Army life to college administrator were managed with the impeccable timing that only God can effect: I was on the job at Asbury less than six weeks after I had decided to retire from the Army.

Our house had briefly been on the market in South Carolina before we had decided to lease it in order to build equity. A new executive in the community had agreed to a lease-purchase option, paperwork had been signed, and we had felt like the matter had been settled. Now all of this was about to change.

One morning I was awakened by a call from an old friend. "Harvey, will you sell me your house?"

Rick and Lilliet Garrison were good friends who had lived across the street in Germany. Now they were returning to the States, assigned to Fort Jackson. Marilyn and I had hosted them several times while they were looking for a place to buy, and they had finally put a contract on a home. However, that night, they had decided that they had purchased the wrong house.

"We never really had peace about it but just couldn't find anything better. But we were both up all night and agreed that the peace of God was resting on your home. We believe that's the house we're supposed to have."

Rick kept talking. "You never said anything about it, so we didn't think it was an option. But I drove to your house before day-break, sat in your driveway, and prayed that the Lord would give us a second chance on this one. Tell me, is there any way you can get out of the lease and sell us your house? I'll pay whatever it takes to be in the center of God's will."

There was one possibility. The lease had a clause making it contingent upon good references from previous landlords. Our future tenant had seemed the perfect candidate, so I had never checked his references. Much to my surprise, a previous landlord in Texas told a horror story convincing me to cancel the lease. After instructing my lawyer to execute the cancellation, I called Rick back and rejoiced. When closing time came, Rick saved $30,000 by purchasing our home, and we made a profit of $197 on the sale. God gave both our families a blessing.

We also faced a housing challenge in Kentucky. The Wilmore market was so small that houses were frequently sold by word of mouth before signs were placed in the yard, but Father seemed to reserve a large older home for us—directly across from the northern edge of the campus. It was a huge old home: fifty-seven hundred square feet of Bedford limestone. From the moment we walked through the front door, I knew that this was to be "the Brown House."

Originally built by an old Holiness musical evangelist, Byron Crouse, the house had never been locked. Missionaries from around the world had lodged there, and countless college students and preachers had sat around the kitchen table telling stories of God's grace and praying for the salvation of the lost. Over the years, young students in seminary and college had resided in three small apartments that were part of the house. The old place had a rich spiritual history, and we were going to continue the tradition.

I reported to the college, in-processed as a new employee, and immediately went to Dartmouth for a conference. By the first of August, the family had joined me in our new "old Kentucky home."

I enjoyed strolling under a lush green canopy of walnut and maple as I made the three-minute walk to my office. I loved the mornings—the scent of freshness resting gently on dew-laden grass, with only a cardinal's song breaking the quiet. I wondered whether Adam had felt like this during his morning walks in the Garden. I was going to tread this path daily in the weeks and months to come. Would my excitement about being back at Asbury ever change? I hoped not.

Those first few weeks were busy ones as the college readied itself for the arrival of the new school year. Much of my time was spent planning meetings, having personal conferences with other faculty and staff, and setting up my office. Once the students were back, the whole community seemed to experience excitement and new life, much like I was feeling in my own return to Wilmore.

The vast majority of the twelve-hundred young men and women who made up the student body were very committed believers, and many had already been involved in short-term mission trips. Quite a few were gifted musicians. Most radiated personal faith combined with an unbridled enthusiasm for the things of God. As I moved across campus, I saw reflected in the faces of these students an image of myself as a young man twenty-six years earlier. But one thing was becoming more and more apparent—the reflection had been significantly blurred by time…and sin.

The longer I was at Asbury with these marvelous young Christians, the more I developed a creeping awareness that my interior world had become a desert wasteland. I was holding good, solid, biblically orthodox truth, but the life of the Spirit was a distant memory. I realized that I was living and proclaiming a memory—that there was no currency in my spirituality. I rapidly discovered that I was barren and bereft of any joy—real joy—in Christ.

In some ways I had become a caricature of many churchmen I had met as a young believer. As a new child of God, I initially

turned to church leaders—primarily preachers—looking for someone that understood and identified with my newfound enthusiasm
for the Savior. But frequently what I discovered was a "professional
Christian": someone paid to do church but lacking passion and fire.
They appreciated what was happening in my life, but rarely did I
sense a resonance between us as I talked about my new birth or
what I was discovering in the Word.

After college and graduate school, I had learned how to adapt to
the "system." Being United Methodist meant that I was part of a
theological mixed-bag denomination, since we contained the full
range of fighting fundamentalists to outspoken liberals. Clergy
most frequently tilted toward the liberal view, while congregations
tended towards conservatism. Yet no matter where you found yourself on the theological spectrum, you had to fit in if you wanted to
succeed. Cookie-cutter clergy stood the best chance of thriving in
the church, so if you had fire, it was best to keep it the fireplace.
Don't move far from the middle or move too fast. Be mainstream
and respectable, learn the ropes, don't ask too many questions, and
certainly don't rock the boat. Play by the rules, and the system will
take care of you.

Although I didn't set out to replace passion for ministry with
professionalism, nonetheless I gradually drifted toward the center
of acceptability. I saw no developing conflict between being baptized by
the system and doing effective ministry. On the contrary, I told myself,
what better place to be responsive to the Lord than as a person of
influence in a eight-and-a-half million member denomination?

Over the years I had honed the mechanics of ministry to a sharp
edge: I knew when to speak a word of comfort or just sit silently by,
nodding my head in response. Sermons were carefully crafted to
capture and hold listener attention, designed to peak at the right
moment to achieve the desired effect. Additional training qualified
me as a staff and parish development consultant. I was recognized
among peers for these gifts, and evaluations by my superiors consistently lauded my preaching skill and ministry performance.

But I had been substituting my own efforts, energies, and education for the leadership and presence of the Holy Spirit. Not that these are necessarily mutually exclusive, but I fell into a trap Jesus referred to as having a form of godliness but denying its power. I had been living in a world of self-directed ministry.

As I compared myself to other known clergy, I found it easy to consider myself better than they. I regularly saw my preaching result in people being saved or touched by the Lord and interpreted these responses as God's blessings on my ministry. I didn't factor that the Lord was honoring the proclamation of His Word, and not necessarily the proclaimer. I was mistaking God's mercy for His favor.

Another significant dynamic was at work within me. A problem of lust and pornography that I normally repressed was still regularly rearing its head and leading me to feel powerless against sin. The cyclical trap described by Paul in Romans 7—wanting to do right but not being able to—had led to hopelessness. Inwardly I longed for a deliverance that always seemed just out of reach. I had bargained and pleaded with God, promising Him that if He would remove the compulsion, I would never again give in. Yet I always fell back into a cycle of addictive behavior. I was trapped.

The Fort Monmouth chapel had once hosted Christian balladeer Don Francisco for a concert. During one interlude, he had referred to how Jesus had delivered him from an addiction to pornography. I had wanted so much to talk with him afterwards, or even call him on the phone and ask him to pray for me, but the shame of my sinfulness had kept me from bringing it to the light. I had wanted to have God deal with me privately so that no one else would have to know. I was important in the church, at least in my own eyes, and had felt that I should be above and beyond such behavior. I'd just have to work it out on my own. No one else needed to know.

Over the years I had made uneasy peace with the monster: Fight it, push it back, give in when you can't stand it any more, then hope that God would forgive me one more time. Although Asbury

College believed in a doctrine of sanctification and holiness, I never proclaimed the doctrine as such because I couldn't find it working in my own life. Much of what I saw in holiness circles was people tied up in "not's": it's *not* right to do this, it's *not* right to do that. I longed for a holiness of life that wasn't based on striving. I wanted to be free but held out little hope that anything would ever be fundamentally different until I got to Heaven.

The more I came to know the students, the more I heard about what Jesus was doing in their lives. So many had fantastic testimonies of God's grace and deliverance. Some had experienced trauma and brokenness beyond my comprehension, yet the Lord had rescued them and set them free. Others had overcome addictions and were now completely liberated. As I listened to them talk about their love for Jesus, I began to sense a softening in my heart that resembled a slightly opened window through which the breeze could enter. Something was stirring deep within me.

I also became aware of a renewing stream moving across the face of the church. People in Wilmore had been touched by it. Six months prior to our coming to the community, the local United Methodist Church was the scene of a conference entitled "Light the Fire."

As newcomers to the area, we had quickly heard about the event—pro and con. Randy Clark had been invited by a nearby parachurch ministry to conduct a series of meetings, along with guest speakers Dr. Guy Chevreau and Jim Goll. By all accounts, the meetings were considered by many to be "chaotic" and resulted in significant division in both the academic and church communities. In hushed and almost scandalous tones, well-meaning folks told us about attendees barking and falling on the floor. Excesses, according to these heralds, were the norm. Some people were even coached on when and how to be slain in the spirit. I did discover, though, that the accounts were not firsthand: The vast majority of naysayers were merely repeating what they had heard from others.

Other people had attended the meetings and found significant encounters with God. Some had faith restored, others were healed, some saw broken relationships mended, and still others experienced a new understanding of the Father heart of God and His special love for them.

Position papers read at faculty forums described how these meetings could not have been from God. Suspicion coursed like a flash flood through a narrow ravine, and the academic community that frequently discussed the theological concept of "perfect love" demonstrated very little. Battle lines were clearly drawn. The executive director of a well-known evangelistic ministry lost his job because he attended the conference against the wishes of the organization's president. When I spoke to him, he said, "Harvey, how could I judge something unless I saw it for myself? I just want more of God. I really don't care what He uses for a delivery system."

I was perplexed over how so much antagonism and hostility could be directed towards a Christian conference in a town like Wilmore. Here were Asbury College and Asbury Theological Seminary—institutions that over the last century had experienced some fantastic outpourings of the Spirit of God.

Having worked in the Army's trans-denominational setting for so long, I was not very concerned about various kinds of religious expression. I didn't think that people should be confined to a religious or theological ghetto where everyone in the "hood" had to be like everyone else. I was very comfortable in both liturgical and free church settings, and I had worked with and for Christians from many different backgrounds and worship styles. As long as no property was destroyed and as long as Jesus was close to the center of what was going on, any form of worship was alright with me.

In many ways, my position was a clear reflection of Methodist-founder John Wesley, who wrote in one of his standard sermons, "So far as in conscience you can (while retaining your own manner of worship) join with me in the work of God; let us go on hand in

John Wesley quote

hand."[1] Wesley urged tolerance and flexibility toward others within the Christian family who differed on points not essential to the core of the faith. "Every wise man, therefore, will allow others the same liberty of thinking which he desires they should allow him…. He bears with those who differ from him, and only asks him with whom he desires to unite in love that single question, 'Is your heart right, as my heart is with your heart?' "[2]

In a town where being "Wesleyan" was so important, I wondered why we couldn't model this basic level of tolerance so foundational to our theological and biblical roots. The uproar over a single set of meetings seemed terribly unhealthy. If the folks at the local Methodist church didn't like what happened when they lent someone their building, all they needed to do was not allow the building to be used in that manner again, and then let things rest. There was no need to beat a dead horse. *Let's be loving*, I thought. *It's over. Let it go.*

But then there were those people who sensed God's presence in the meetings. Their conversational tone was altogether different, lacking the scared and hostile edge I heard much too frequently in detractors' comments. These voices were reasoned and passionate, and (to me) reflected a much more graceful and conciliatory tone. These people seemed to have been profoundly touched by God, and their lives began to touch me.

Perhaps none touched me any more than that of Jeff James. Jeff was Assistant Director of Physical Plant at Asbury College. When I first saw him, he was playing bass guitar in the praise band for an early semester college chapel service. I was captured by the smooth style and quick hands of this musician. Yet another quality attracted me even more: He was worshiping on his instrument. I soon learned what a special brother he was.

---

1. John Wesley, *Standard Sermons*, (London: Epworth Press, 1981), p. 141.
2. Ibid., pp. 132-133.

Late one afternoon I bumped into Jeff as he was leaving the president's office. I introduced myself and, since my office was immediately across the hall from the president's, invited him to step in for a visit. For the next two and a half hours we talked and shared about the Lord. The longer we talked, the more I sensed that a special grace rested upon him. There are some people with whom you get along with right away: Jeff was one of those people for me.

After several minutes of preliminary background questions, we talked about local church fellowships and spiritual happenings in the community. Jeff told me that he attended the Vineyard Church and that, although many people thought it an outgrowth of the "Light the Fire Conference," its launch was only coincidental to the meetings. The church had been planned for almost two years, but the conference had become a watershed on the spiritual map of Wilmore.

"I've heard a number of things, most said with a good bit of feeling, about the two new churches started here and how they've torn up the community," I said. "Are you all really like that?"

"No," he smiled, slowly shaking his head. "We're not out stealing sheep or putting down anyone. It's just that we want to worship in a style and freedom that goes beyond 'Sunday morning as usual' church. Vineyard-style seems to express best what we're feeling in terms of renewal. We don't aim to split or put down anything."

"That's not what I've heard," I responded.

"You'd be amazed at both the open hostility and cold indifference we've received from some folks here in town. People who have known us for years—people that were close family friends— now treat me like I have some kind of contagious disease."

There was visible pain in Jeff's eyes. "I love these people. I was raised here. Had them for Sunday School teachers, grew up with their kids. But now I'm an outcast because I associate with believers who are more demonstrative and have some different under-standings of the Spirit's work."

I thought of how Army chapels nurtured great respect for be-lievers from different traditions. But obviously, this wasn't "Fort Wilmore" but a civilian community. There was no commander who would call the town together, tell everyone to be nice, serve the Lord, love the brethren, and then get back to building the King-dom. This was a theological and experiential battleground where many were more concerned with strengthening their positions than seeking a truce and pursuing peace. I sensed how deeply Jeff had been hurt in this battle. The pathos was plain. Old relationships had been wrecked because his religious experience was considered outside the norm. He was no longer mainstream.

The more we talked, the more I became convinced of a deep and abiding gracefulness in Jeff that was both appealing and threat-ening. Appealing because it reflected the winsomeness of the Holy Spirit cultivating fruit in a brother's life, threatening because it dis-armed any arguments I might have wanted to construct against the behavior of renewal folks. If what I saw in Jeff's life was the result of some shaking and falling, then maybe all of us (myself included) could have used a dose of it. Jeff was obviously in love with Jesus.

A friend had once defined a fanatic as "someone who loved Je-sus more than you do." If that were the case, then Jeff certainly ap-peared to be a fanatic.

I had known Jeff's father during my earlier days in Wilmore and had found him (like Jeff) to be pleasant and affable. Although "Penny" James and I had not spent much time together, I felt that it would be a different story with his son. I looked forward to the next time Jeff and I would be together.

fanatic defined

6

A Growing Hunger

Blessed are those who hunger and thirst for righteousness, for they will be filled. (Jesus)

As fall left a colorful imprint on the hardwoods, Wilmore's children of renewal were leaving their imprint on me. Everywhere I turned, I was talking with old and new friends living on the cutting edge of faith. In comparison, my faith seemed dull and old next to their vibrancy and vitality.

During the next few months, over many cups of coffee at our little Cozy Cafe, I questioned and probed, debated and discussed, dissected and analyzed the current renewal. I was intrigued not so much by any phenomena associated with the Holy Spirit's presence (although that was a significant part of the discussions) but with the resulting fruit in the lives of persons with whom I talked. They were so alive and in love with the Lord that their joy was contagious. Being with them was like eating fresh tropical fruit picked from a tree, compared with opening a can of grapefruit slices. It was all the difference in the world, although both fruit came from the same source.

I renewed a friendship with Dr. Stephen Seamands, whom I had met at a college reunion weekend several years previously. I had known of him through stories Marilyn had told of growing up in

Wilmore—stories that included kids sledding down Moody's Hill and then warming themselves by the fire at the Seamands' home. In another way, I felt like I knew Steve because his father—well-known author Dr. David Seamands—was the beloved pastor of the Wilmore Church when I was a college student. It was easy for me to transfer to Steve some of the great respect I felt for his dad. Like his father, Steve was also a seminary professor and author.

One day Steve joined me for lunch. I had appreciated the few times that we had been together and looked forward to knowing him better. During our luncheon conversation, I discovered that he too had been touched by renewal. Here was a scholar—one of the most popular professors at the seminary—sitting across the table from me and describing a powerful inner healing he had experienced while lying on the floor, slain in the Spirit!

I was really impressed now. Steve had all the credentials and competence necessary to impress anyone in an academic environment, yet was talking about a personal experience that defied fully rational explanation. This mystical encounter with the Lord at the "Light the Fire Conference" had touched an area of his life previously out of reach.

I threw questions at him with machine-gun rapidity. What had happened? What had it felt like? How did you know it was the Lord?

Steve answered my sincere questions patiently and honestly. There was no attempt to persuade or convince, just a candid unveiling of his heart. His transparency was disarming as he shared some deep hurts from childhood. He had experienced a tough time growing up on the mission field in India. Because of the remote location of his parents' mission, the better part of Steve's early years were spent in a boarding school hundreds of miles away from his family. As a little boy he didn't understand the sacrifices his parents were making to follow the Lord; his inner child interpreted separation as rejection. The ten years in India had left deeply repressed scars that the Holy Spirit had miraculously healed.

I was duly impressed with what Steve had shared. His testimony of God's work was especially significant because of my desire to accept only credible information. When describing myself, I frequently would say that I "was a skeptic but not a doubter." By this, I meant that credibility and verification were essential before I could accept information or reports on an event. All too often in Christian circles, I encountered information repeated as fact that I knew was erroneous—everything from Madeline Murray O' Hare's supposed petition to the FCC to eliminate all Christian broadcasting to the preposterous lie that Proctor and Gamble was owned by the church of Satan. I had listened to established preachers parrot illustrations they picked up from others, without researching the data's accuracy.

I commonly heard someone underscoring a preaching point by dispensing good-sounding but ill-informed academic knowledge. I'll never forget the embarrassment I felt for one national speaker when I heard him describing how grapevines were grown, in order to pinpoint what Jesus meant in John 15 about the vine and branches. Although he understood biblical principle, it was clear that the man didn't have a clue about viticulture, and this misunderstanding could have destroyed his credibility in the minds of unbelievers. Someone who tended vines might have reasonably said, "If this man is wrong about how vines grow, how do I know he's right about God?"

The Lord Jesus continued to bring people like Jeff and Steve into my life. Among others, Mark Nysewander and Steve Beard had opportunities to share with me the exciting things that the Holy Spirit was accomplishing in and through them. At Steve Seamands' invitation, I began meeting with some brothers before work on Wednesday mornings to pray. Most of these men had been touched by the current renewal, and I quietly and increasingly found myself drawn toward that spiritual river.

The more I listened to what these people were sharing, the more I yearned to have God redig the old wells in my life. In combination with the credible witness of brothers and sisters who were part of the local renewal, these experiences forced me to consider the following proposition: Would I remain content to stand on the banks of the stream of renewal and applaud those who splashed joyfully in the waters? The waters were turbulent, and turbulence certainly stirs up a lot of mud. Or would I jump into the waters, regardless of their turbulence, and trust that the buoyancy of Christ's Spirit would keep me afloat?

I was wrestling with my continued ordination in the United Methodist Church during our General Conference in Denver in April 1996. Fifteen United Methodist Bishops had stunned everyone on the second day by issuing a formal statement endorsing full ordination and acceptance of homosexuals. Although this action carried no weight in terms of the church's official position, it did signal a clear divergence from Scripture and our historical position, revealing how far our church had drifted from the truth. Deeply grieved, I was considering what steps to take if our church's legislative body followed these bishops. As a result, I was enlisting people nationwide to pray that I would respond correctly during this crisis. I decided to call Gary and Anni Shelton and ask them to pray.

I had fallen in love with the Sheltons one evening during a serendipitous meeting in the cafe in our little town. As Marilyn and I were leaving the restaurant, we had passed a table where Jeff and Donna James were dining with a couple unknown to us, who were introduced as, Gary and Anni, visiting Wilmore from St. Louis. Gary had led worship during the "Light the Fire Conference" the previous February and had returned to our area for a visit. We pulled up a chair and began to talk.

That night's gathering was a study in contrasts. I, with my thinning hair and military-style haircut, sat next to Gary with his Absolom-like hair hanging halfway down his back. My college administrator suit differed from his jeans, T-shirt, and leather jacket.

But we hit it off right away. In moments, we were laughing and cutting up as if we were old friends getting together after a long absence. We drank cappuccino until the cafe closed, then relocated to our home for fellowship into the early morning hours. I broke out my guitars, and we took turns sharing music and singing. I had not heard the renewal music that Gary shared, but we also discovered that he and Anni had never heard the old gospel songs that were part of our spiritual tradition. They were children of renewal, saved as adults, and hadn't grown up in traditional churches. When I sang "Love Lifted Me," tears flowed down Gary's and Anni's cheeks. "That's the most beautiful song…it's really our story," declared Anni. As they left our house, I knew that we were now good friends—friends who would be together again.

We stayed in touch by phone, talking every week or two and hoping that our paths would soon cross again. It was only natural that I contacted them to pray for me about my denomination. Their detachment from Methodism would allow them freedom to seek the Lord in prayer without being biased by inside knowledge. As far as I knew, they didn't know a Methodist from a Mormon. I called and shared my turmoil.

During our phone conversation, Anni invited me to come to St. Louis for a meeting. "Next month we're having a conference out here called 'Praying Down the Fire.' Randy Clark is hosting it, and there will be some terrific speakers. Why don't you see if you can come? Gary's leading worship, and you can see firsthand what a renewal event is like." She continued. "Jeff James is going to come out and play bass for Gary's band. I'm sure you could ride with him."

I was surprised that I had a week completely clear on my calendar and, after coordinating a ride with my friend Jeff James, decided to make the trip.

For two weeks prior to the conference, I found myself periodically weeping quietly for no apparent reason. I began to pray that the Lord would redig those old wells and cause me to rediscover my first love. Two events led me to believe that our Lord might indeed be working in the interior parts of my life.

Ten days prior to going to St. Louis, I accompanied Steve Seamands to Kingsport, Tennessee, where he was speaking at a gathering of United Methodists from East Tennessee and Southwest Virginia. Going with him gave us time to discuss the recently adjourned United Methodist General Conference, as well as what the Lord was doing in the world. I was also excited about the trip because I had pastored in that area of the country prior to entering the Army. Inexplicably, when we were about forty-five miles from our destination, I began to weep. I wept almost continually for the next twenty-four hours. When we reached the church where the meeting was to be held, my previously tan slacks were now dotted with tear stains.

During worship, I found myself kneeling at my pew in adoration of our risen Lord. I had not given myself so freely in worship for years—I rarely knelt at all. I had told myself that playing basketball and jumping out of airplanes had beaten my knees to the point that I shouldn't kneel on them. Yet falling to my knees during worship was the most natural response that I could make. When I returned home the next night, I told Marilyn that I felt like I had genuinely worshipped more in the last twenty-four hours than I had in the last ten years.

The second event was a trip to prison. Steve Luce, Chairman of the Board for Bill Glass Ministries, invited me to spend the weekend in prison as a volunteer counselor for a Bill Glass "Weekend of Champions." We spent almost three days at the Kentucky State Reformatory witnessing to inmates about Christ's love and sharing the gospel. I saw hundreds of inmates touched for the Lord, and had the chance to personally lead seven men to the Savior. Each time I prayed the "sinner's prayer" with someone, I felt my own heart stirred again just as I had when praying it for myself years before. It was as if I were reliving my own introduction to Jesus through the conversions of others. My zeal for personal evangelism was re-ignited.

We left for St. Louis after I returned from the prison ministry. Jeff and I spent the morning at the college, then joined Steve Sawyer, a portrait artist from nearby Versailles, for the trip to Missouri. I believed that the questions I had about renewal in its current expression were soon going to be answered. Personally, I was not inclined to chase after spiritual thrill rides. But what compelled me to go was my quest for answers to three overriding questions about renewal: What? So what? Now what?

These three questions really expressed my own heart. What was it about? What was the meaning, both personally for me as well as for the larger body of Christ? And, in the long run, how would I respond after seeing renewal firsthand?

7

When God Strikes the Match

Therefore, since we are receiving a kingdom that cannot be shaken, let us be thankful, and so worship God acceptably with reverence and awe, for our "God is a consuming fire" (Hebrews 12:28-29).

When I arrived in St. Louis, I explicitly told the Lord that I was seeking no special experience. My only goal was to genuinely know Him better and love Him more. If I were to have an "experience," that was okay, but even if I returned home without experiencing any phenomenon or manifestation, as long as I loved Christ more it would have been worth the trip and the expense. I was being totally honest with God about what I expected. Opinions and description by others were no longer sufficient: I just had to see for myself.

In regard to my three questions, the "So what?" was answered during the pre-conference pastors' meeting. As a hundred or more pastors gathered in a side room at the Regal Riverfront Hotel, Randy Clark described renewal hitting the Church as waves breaking upon the seashore. Renewal was not a single splash but rather a series of visitations by the Holy Spirit to accomplish what God desired. Randy described the outpouring first experienced in Toronto as the first wave of renewal of a dry Church, and that successive waves of renewal would equip us to minister salvation to the nations—to take the message of God's love for the lost to the ends of the earth.

I was impressed. Here was one of the key renewal leaders saying things that were resonating with what was going on in my world. My passions for the lost were as high as they had ever been. The softening in my heart, as well as the basics of one-on-one prison evangelism, had moved me to a renewed compassion for those who did not know the Savior. And Randy Clark sounded as if he had an evangelist's heart, rather than one of a feel-good, get-a-religious-buzz preacher. There was no "just-bless-me" club here: I saw real hearts for the lost.

During the final moments of the pastors' meeting, the Lord really got my attention. Gary Shelton was leading us in a chorus after Randy prayed for the lost, when Fred Grewe (an associate of Randy Clark's) came to the microphone. He said that the Lord had shown him that there were pastors in the room who were struggling continually with pornography and masturbation. He invited those desiring freedom to come to the back for prayer.

My mind began to spin. Could it be that the Lord would finally set me free? Maybe this was something for others. I hesitated. I had prayed about this problem before but had slipped easily into old patterns of destructive behavior. I had begged God for deliverance while shedding tears on altar rails on three continents. Why would this do any good? And why expose my sin in front of others? I was a professional Christian and a leader in my circles. Perhaps I could just deal with this on my own and no one would ever have to know.

I waited a few moments, hestitating to move. When I glanced over my shoulder and saw a good number of men already waiting, I realized that I'd have no place to stand if I didn't go soon. I hurried back, hoping to be invisible in the crowd. I was the last in the line of respondents. After a few minutes, Fred stood in front of me and stared intently. I felt as if he could see directly into my heart.

"You've been unable to fulfill the exceedingly high expectations in your life," he said, "and are retreating into a fantasy world for relief and solace." Wham! His words nailed me right between the eyes. This was it. God knew ME!

Although I would have never described it as such, I knew that God had me figured out. (For one, my personality type on the Myers-Briggs Personality Type Inventory is one of the most self-critical of the sixteen.) After he finished speaking, Fred gently placed his hands on my head and took authority over this in my life. I slipped quietly into a peaceful state of rest as someone behind me eased me to the floor. Waves of mercy washed over me. I knew a miraculous healing was taking place.

While I was on the floor, the Lord reminded me of the time when I was twelve and on a class trip to Washington D.C. It was there that my friend Pete had introduced me to masturbation and where this practice had become a regular escape from loneliness and unfulfilled expectations in my life. But now I was free. No longer were we dealing with symptoms. God was dealing a death blow to the root of my problem by taking me back to the source.

Yet there was more. The issue of pornography as a supporting actor in this lurid drama paraded before me. Eight years earlier, while away from home for a nine-week Army training course, I had rented an x-rated video tape. "I'm just curious," I told myself. "What real harm can come from this? I'm away from home in another state where no one knows me. I'll only do this once to satisfy my curiosity, and that will be it." But it wasn't.

Not only did the images from that movie replay in my mind, but a stronghold had been established that resulted in my having to repeatedly fight the same battles. I had allowed the enemy a beachhead in my life that my accuser continued to exploit, with raiding parties whose mission it was to keep me harassed, distracted, and confused. I might beat back one assault only to find that devilish snipers were keeping me from effectively winning this battle. I was waging an internal guerrilla warfare against allied enemies of masturbation and pornography. Only occasional lulls in the battle allowed me rest, but I was always fearful of another ambush just around the corner.

Because of this internal war, the victories I experienced always had for me a certain tainted feeling. Sure, God used my preaching and people's lives were changed. But because of my private world of sinful failures, I was continually plagued with guilt and condemnation—real guilt and condemnation—that gnawed at me like a hungry vulture devouring a carcass.

At least, it did until God overwhelmed me with His love.

As I reflected on what Father was doing in my life, I realized that it was very similar to a wrestling match with the Lord. But He had changed the rules to "no holds barred," promptly pinned me to the mat with His love, then pulled me to my feet and raised my hands in the air while declaring me the victor. Glory to His marvelous Name!

Needless to say, I was fully open to "renewal" by the time the conference formally began that evening. God had already done a powerful work in my interior world. I wanted to see with my own eyes what His work looked like in a corporate setting.

The grand ballroom of the Regal Riverfront Hotel was magnificently decorated. Three huge crystal chandeliers hanging from the ornate ceiling cast a soft glow over eleven hundred chairs. Conferees mingled and visited with one another as Gary Shelton and the worship team moved to the platform. After some preliminary announcements were made, Gary struck a few chords on his guitar. "Praying Down the Fire" had begun.

As the congregation entered worship, I saw the various manifestations and exuberance of which I had heard—answering the "What?" question concerning renewal. Although there was some strange stuff going on, I really wasn't bothered. To gain a panoramic view, I moved to one end of the ballroom. Jumping, dancing, shouting, whirling, jerking. Wonderful music. And a sudden awareness that this may more closely approximate the celebration before the Throne than our liturgical singing of the doxology on Sunday mornings. I wished I could have seen it from God's perspective because to me—earthbound as I was—it was altogether lovely.

I had been in stadiums around the country, standing among 60,000 people exhuberant because some overgrown adolescent had kicked a ball through the uprights. I had jumped and shouted, given high-fives to strangers, danced in the aisles with fellow fans because my team was winning. The question came to my mind while I observed conference worshipers: Why should not the children of God equally celebrate Him who has conquered sin and death? Was God any less deserving of our unrestrained joy?

There were some things I found distracting or excessive. And quite probably there were displays of joy with their source in the fallible man rather than the perfect Spirit. But in the grand scheme of the universe, I think the Lord would prefer our exuberance rather than our politely constrained religious rituals. My paradigm was shifting.

I was standing on the riverbanks watching children splash gleefully in the waters of renewal. Would I be content to watch, or would I jump in with them? The question didn't linger very long. I had been released from the weight of my sin at the afternoon pastors' session, and nothing remained to hold me back. I was free in a way that I had never been before. I joined the dance. I threw my head back and laughed at what it must look like to a loving Father. Here I was, middle-aged and respectable, acting like a little kid.

At that moment I felt that my heavenly Father was dancing with me just as I had done with my children when they were in preschool. Sometimes we would put music on the stereo and dance around the coffee table, laughing. I thought nothing of dancing, hopping, and skipping with them in their childish innocence, since these silly little dances with my children were precious times. And here I was, Father's child, trying my own new dance, all the while sensing that my Father was probably dancing with me—and enjoying it just as much. I was free to express the joy of my heart with my whole being. And no one was saying "You shouldn't act that way."

Certainly not God. He's the Lord of the dance. He's a dancing God. It's hard to describe the dynamic of what happened inside me as the conference continued. Although I had been in professional ministry for twenty-five years, I never felt released to "act out" in the physical dimension what I was sensing in the spiritual and emotional. The ability to abandon myself in acts of praise and worship was like opening the flood gates of a dam that had been holding back waters of rejoicing. At times, my praise gushed out in torrents. I wanted nothing but to be in the presence of the King and praise Him.

In the atmosphere of joyous praise I could set aside my inhibitions and do just that. At one point I found myself standing on my chair, arms uplifted, and psalming at the top of my voice as James Dillingham laid down hot guitar licks to one of the praise songs. And nobody could really hear me because my voice was just one in a multitude of a thousand that were focused on glorifying Him who sat on the Throne.

Kim, one of the hotel supervisors, had been especially helpful in resolving some difficulties with our room, and she had made additional efforts to ensure that our stay was pleasant. Kim was in her early twenties and reminded me of my oldest daughter. After interacting with her several times at the desk, I found myself praying for an opportunity to share Christ with her. On Thursday night, I stopped by the front desk and thanked her again for her kindness and professionalism, then asked her if she might have a few moments for me near the end of her shift. She said she would meet me in the lobby after she had finished some paperwork.

My intention was to introduce her to Jesus if she did not know Him. As soon as I began to share, a smile crossed her face. "I know Him too," she beamed. "And you were so nice when there was the problem with your room, I thought for sure that you must be a believer." She then shared with me that she would be graduating from college the following Saturday.

"Are you planning to make tourism and trade a career?" I asked.

"No," she replied, "I've been wondering whether the Lord was calling me to the mission field. It's something I've really been wrestling with lately. I want to do whatever it is that He wants me to do, but I'm just not sure."

I told Kim that the meeting I was attending was a Christian gathering and asked if she would like to go pray with some folks in the ballroom. When we arrived downstairs, the scene looked as if a mortar round had landed nearby—there were bodies everywhere. The few still standing were grouped together.

I wanted to place Kim with some sisters because it was important not to be involved in one-on-one ministry with a young woman. Although I had opened the doors for her, I was very sensitive to the potential spiritual dangers of solo ministry. As we moved through the room, I saw Judy Wright and introduced Kim. Still on her knees, Judy extended a hand in greeting to Kim and chuckled sheepishly. "Excuse me for not standing up. My legs don't seem to be working right now. Would you mind kneeling down here with me?"

Judy and her husband Robert pastored the Vineyard Christian Fellowship in Cape Girardeau, Missouri, and Anni Shelton had introduced us early in the conference. I felt that Judy was a good person for Kim to connect with. I smiled inside as I watched Kim—still in her hotel blazer, tie, and name badge—kneel with Judy on the floor and begin prayer. I rested my hand on Kim's shoulder.

While she was praying, Mark Endres—Randy Clark's conference coordinator—came up and began to pray. I told him about Kim's calling. Mark replied that he was about to pray for Kim's choice between the two paths that faced her. Before Mark began to pray, however, Judy prayed the same thing verbatim. Kim collapsed into Judy's arms and was laid onto the floor while Mark and Judy continued to "soak" her in prayer.

As I watched this scene, I couldn't help but realize how merciful our Father is. He wanted Kim to understand specifically that He not only knew what her heart's desire was, but He wanted to communicate this message plainly to her.

Carol Arnott was nearby kneeling in prayer for someone—I recognized her from an earlier session where she and her husband John (pastors of the Toronto Airport Christian Fellowship) were welcomed in the meetings. When she finished praying, I knelt beside her and introduced myself. I wanted to move beyond observation to participation. God had done so much for me in such a short span of time that I wanted to pass it along and help free others. But I really didn't want to appear weird.

"Carol," I said, "I would like for you to pray that God would impart me with just enough so that I can impart it to others." The prayer seemed safe enough. I didn't need or want bells and whistles, lightning and thunder. I just sought a release of Holy Spirit power for ministry.

She complied, praying words reflecting my desire. "But one other thing you need to know," she said, flashing a delightful grin, "I'm going to stalk you for the rest of the conference. Every time that I see you or think about you, I will pray that Father will pour out more of His extravagant love on you. Be blessed!" I felt like I was.

I returned to Kim, now standing. I felt an overwhelming desire to pray for her. I truly believed, because of my own experience of being slain in the Spirit the previous day, as well as my observation of others, that this was a common phenomenon in renewal ministry. But I had also observed during the process of laying on hands that some persons were either pushed or pressed down. I recoiled from this idea and wanted no part of it. Ministry wasn't in falling down. It was in what the Holy Spirit was doing in the inner person, regardless of whether they were standing, lying, or sitting. If there were to be any demonstration of power, I wanted it to be God and Him alone.

So I told the Lord, "If You were to choose to manifest Yourself through me, Father, I want there to be no confusion or self-delusion. No heavy-handedness, no little pushes to 'help' the Spirit do His work. If You choose to use me, make it so plain and irrefutable that no one will doubt that it is indeed the work of Your Spirit." I decided to not lay hands on anyone during the ministry of prayer.

As I began to pray, I held my hands over Kim's head. A visible serenity enveloped her, and after the prayer she remained motionless for a long time. She looked at me and said, "I've never felt like this in my life."

"What did you feel?" I was curious.

"As if my mind had emptied of everything and that there was a very heavy pressure bearing down on my head." I replied that I hadn't been touching her, and she said that she knew that. I asked if the pressure had been a negative kind of thing. She shook her head. No.

I asked if I could pray for her again, and she agreed. Once more I placed my hands over her head, and this time prayed, "Father, impart the gift of Your Spirit's power and special presence to Kim, in the name of Jesus." Immediately Kim fell backwards and rested in the Spirit for an hour. When the ballroom finally closed for the night, Gary, Anni, and I had to assist a staggering Kim from the room. New wine is apparently heady stuff, even for hotel staff.

The manifest power of the Spirit was shown twice more the following morning—once as I stood behind a woman in a group awaiting prayer. I was curious if falling down in the Spirit was a response precipitated by suggestion. In other words, would a person be slain in the Spirit if they didn't necessarily know they were being prayed for? I couldn't get rid of the thought: What would happen if I held my hands over this lady's head while she unknowingly was looking elsewhere?

I held my hand over her head and began to pray in my spirit. The Lord seemed to impress on me the need to pray for her against a spirit of rejection. As I began to speak, she collapsed suddenly and rather dramatically into my arms, so quickly that I almost dropped her.

I laid her on the floor and began to weep. God was using me. Something new was taking place that was both wonderful and frightening. I wondered at the power of God and His willingness to impart it to His children. I was frightened at the prospect of being entrusted with such a powerful gift. I felt somewhat like an astronaut who, strapped into the centrifuge in flight school, was learning just how much "G-force" he could take. But the "G" in my "G-force" was God.

I also knew that I must pass glory to Jesus immediately after any manifestation. I knew how important it was not to fall prey to the subtle seduction of power—the thought that the manifestation was because of something special within oneself, or that one was somehow responsible for what transpired. This power was God's turf, and I wasn't about to get into a turf war with Him.

On Friday night, Steve Sawyer shared from the platform about how God had touched his life and his art. Steve is a big Peter-esque fellow whose life was tremendously impacted by the "Light the Fire" conference held in Wilmore the previous year. He was really nervous about talking in front of so many people and asked if I would be willing to help him out if he couldn't finish. I told him I would, which really meant "You're on your own, buddy." I knew that he would have to get through this with the Lord's help rather than mine.

Steve stumbled through his testimony in a wonderfully touching way. As he came down from the stage, I met him at the foot of the steps and held him, both of us crying. Randy Clark came beside us and called the congregation to prayer. He prayed for healing in Wilmore since he knew of the rift that had resulted because of renewal, and he prayed for God's favor to rest upon Steve as he continued to learn what it meant to live out his new commitment to

Christ. I stood with my hand on Steve's shoulder as we began to pray for him.

As we prayed, I felt someone touch my left calf. I looked over shoulder and saw Carol Arnott, smiling at me from her seat next to John among the speakers and their wives. Suddenly I realized that my viewing perspective was rapidly changing. Much to my surprise, I was going down in the Spirit.

For the next hour and a half, I was stretched out on the floor at the feet of all the conference speakers and their wives. A friend said that it reminded him of Saturday afternoon WWF Wrestlemania Tag Team World Championships, with yours truly being the poor fellow on the mat. The conference speakers and their wives, simultaneously and in tandem, were praying for me, touching me, imparting anointing and gifts to me, and generally working me over. I was told that this went on continually during praise and worship. I was aware that I was being touched, but the voices, laughter, and general commotion seemed to be several rows away. The sensation was much like what I had felt when I had nitrous oxide administered by a dentist during a root canal. I was aware of what was going on but seemed to be somewhere else at the time. Steve Sawyer sat on the floor next to me the whole time, "guarding the body" so that no one accidentally stepped on me during the exuberance of worship.

While I was on the floor, the Lord gave me a vision:

My home, one block north of Asbury College's main campus, was on fire. Flames were leaping from the dormer windows, running along the gutters and across the gables, and roaring from the windows on the main floor. The front door was a mass of flame.

The fire came out the door and down the sidewalk to the street and into the gutter. Just as if there were some volatile substance in the gutter, the flame ran down the street and turned up Bellevue Street. It jumped across College Avenue and began to roll across the semicircle, which is the front of the campus. As the fire spread down the semicircle, flames licked at the columns of each building. The girl's dorm, the administration building, the classroom building, and Hughes Auditorium (the site of many outpourings of the Holy Spirit, especially the 1970 Asbury Revival) all caught the fire.

The fire turned and went west up Lewis Street to the men's dorms, which immediately burst into flame. It then turned, shot across campus, wound its way through the new apartment style honors dorms, and passed to Kresge Hall, the women's residence hall. The fire then spread down Lexington Avenue between the College and Asbury Seminary, turned and went down Main Street through the small business district and across the tracks.

I then saw my large backyard completely engulfed by huge flames—six, eight, ten feet high. And there were children dancing in the fire! The yard was full of "kids"—adolescents, college students, scruffy drug users and ex-drug-users, the broken, hurting, and wounded children of this world— all skipping, laughing, and dancing in the fire. Every kid in town was there, and my oldest daughter Candace was leading the dance, followed closely by her sister Elizabeth. I celebrated the dance.

I found myself near the presence of the throne, reaching up for the fingertips of Jesus. Straining, straining, reaching... Suddenly a voice said, "Take the sword." A sword resembling a cutlass was in my hand. Immediately I rehearsed a manual of arms within the sword and found myself posted on the stoop outside my front door. Two angels, ministering as flames of fire, were posted as guards on each side of all entrances to my home. My right arm was extended straight out, palm down, with the blade edge held out against all attacks. I was the first line of defense for my castle.

Now I was standing among a faceless needy crowd. I would rub my right hand against the outstretched palm of the left as if to rub off the anointing, then touch those in need of anointing. I would reach my arms around the crowd and pull them inwards, as if in an embrace. In doing so, I sensed that I was drawing them to Jesus.

The vision subsided, and I began to recover. What perplexed me was that I did not then, nor do I now, consider myself a mystic. My natural bent is not toward the mystical—though not a doubter, I still demand hard evidence from which to draw my conclusions. Yet something very profound and mystical had happened to me that I had neither sought nor anticipated. I had received a vision and in part of it found myself in the presence of the glorified Lord. I knew that I was irrevocably changed, essentially different than I was before the vision: the essence of who I was had experienced some kind of dramatic change.

I could never be the same.

After the speaker finished and ministry time began, I walked through the crowd. The manifestation of God's presence was so real that whenever I prayed, God's power would overcome the persons for whom I prayed. I prayed for what seemed like dozens of folk, although I made no attempt to count. Whether I stood behind or in front, whenever I held my hands over someone and imparted the Father's blessing, people would fall, jerk, or heave. Often there was an accompanying specific word in prayer. There was an anointing and unction of the Spirit I had never known, much less anticipated. I was overwhelmed by God's sovereignty and might. I begged Him to remove this from me if in His foreknowledge He knew that I would ever misuse or abuse the power. It remained. Each prayer, each manifestation, became an immediate offering to Jesus for His glory. For His glory alone.

The power continued into Saturday whenever I prayed for someone. On Saturday night I had occasion to pray for Karen Palmer from Madisonville, Kentucky. She and her husband C.D. were members of First Baptist Church and had never attended anything related to renewal or the charismatic movement. They came at the invitation of their friends John and Cindy Roy, and had arrived in St. Louis just the day before.

Karen recounted that when I prayed over her, my hands imparted extreme heat. (And I had never even touched her.) She then reported a great pressure and the sensation of electricity, along with a feeling "like a curling iron" resting on the back of her neck. She fell backward in the Spirit and said that she was enveloped by the brightest light and sense of well-being as she lay on the floor. "I never wanted to get up" she said. "I feel like I have lived life with God in a box—neat and predictable," she continued, "but after what I've experienced He will never fit in that box again."

8

Dancing in the Fire

God creates everything out of nothing—and everything which God is to use He first reduces to nothing. (Sören Kierkegaard)

It seemed that there was no more room for blessing in my life. I had cried, worshipped, and prayed as much as I thought one could possibly do. The coming Sunday worship service at the St. Louis Vineyard would probably be used as a decompression period to help me reenter my normal working world. Much like a scuba diver must decompress after being deep underwater for protracted periods of time, I felt like I too needed decompression. I had gone deep. It had been a long week.

I sat inconspicuously on the outside aisle, about halfway back in the sanctuary. Although the praise and worship was good, my fatigued mind kept drifting towards my family in Kentucky. Still, I anticipated that Jim Goll, the morning's preacher and one of the conference speakers, would keep me awake.

Shortly after beginning his message for the church, he summoned a few people and gave prophetic words over them. Although some of these people had very demonstrative reactions, I wasn't bothered. It was all beginning to seem normal to me by now. What seemed abnormal, however, was an unusual sense of anticipation as he began sharing the following:

"I was out driving once, and the Holy Spirit spoke to me. He said, 'I want you to drive down Blue Ridge Boulevard. I want to show you what I want to give you.' I was driving down this road and passing prominent and traditional church buildings. I went by a Disciples of Christ, by a Nazarene, and by a Bible Fellowship and some others. Then I came up to a United Methodist church building. It was a rather large church and somewhat influential. The Holy Spirit began speaking again and said, 'This is what you could have had.' And then He said, 'I want you to go around, drive into the parking lot, park the car. And then I want you to look at the back of the sign in front of the church building. What is written on the back of the sign is what I am going to give you.' "

I was all ears as Goll continued speaking. Did this "Methodist" connection have something to do with me?

"That was kind of interesting," Jim mused. "Whoever heard of putting something on the back of a reader board church sign? So I drove on down the road. And there was the Methodist church with the front of the sign indicating the times for Sunday school and church. I parked the car. It was night, and I had to get out in order to read the back of the sign. And there was writing in script on the back of the sign. It said, 'The world is my parish—John Wesley.' "

At those words, an electric shock seemed to run up and down my spine.

Jim continued with an increasing intensity in his voice. "Now, I have five releases that I want to call forth, and I want the man back over here, in the purple shirt...."

He was looking directly at me. I was wearing a purple golf shirt.

"Is that your wife there?"

I was really wishing that Marilyn was there. How would she react to all of this? Would she believe me when I tell her?

"Are you by yourself, sir? Right there, yes, you're looking at me...in the purple shirt. Are you by yourself?"

I nodded my head to indicate yes.

"Okay, I'd like you to stand. I think I said something to you, perhaps, and I don't know if you heard it or not. But I said something to you—that you are to look at Guy Chevreau."

I now understood what Jim Goll had said as he stood in front of me the evening before at the conference. He had come to pray for me as I stood in a line of pastors seeking special prayer. In the noise and confusion, I thought he had been praying in tongues. I had no idea that Guy (pronounced 'Ghee') Chevreau was a person. Things were starting to come together. My heart was racing.

"And that which the Lord has done with Guy Chevreau, He is going to do with you. He is going to take the brilliance of academia and He is going to baptize it in His Spirit. And you are going to be a revelatory teacher. And the fire of Wesley is going to be in your fireplace."

I gasped and fell to my knees. There was the fire again.

"And He is going to give it to you, and you are going to carry a message of the fire of sanctification. And you will know that it is not by man's works or by man's efforts, but rather, it is by the cross. And the Lord is going to give to you a revelation of the cross of Christ. You will be one of a new breed of warriors who will be raised up to carry the genetics of those who have gone before us. And you will carry the fire."

I was flat on my face in the floor now, feet under the seats and body in the aisle.

"The Lord is going to cause you to become a trailblazer. He is going to cause you to get, as it were, on a horse and ride...and ride...and ride. And doors are going to open up to you, they're going to open up to you!" He was almost shouting the words.

"There is something, some kind of society, that perhaps you are a part of or will be a part of. Some type of—I don't know the name, but some type of an Aldersgate society that is coming. And it is going to be a renewal flame of fire that is going to carry not only power but a message of sanctification—not by works but by the living flame of the fire of the Lord Jesus Christ. And you are going to be inebriated by this and you are going to be a carrier of it. In the name of Jesus."

People were applauding the word from the Lord and celebrating His revelation. I lay on the floor shaking. Totally overcome by the power of God, I had lost complete control of my upper extremities.

Jim started his trademark chuckle that grew to a laugh. "Now, that man is probably going to need some intercessors." He then prayed, "Okay, Lord, I ask that You raise up intercessors."

There was one final word: "I just speak impact ministries. I don't know what it is, but it will come about at some point. I just say 'Impact ministries' to you."

God had whacked me hard again. After church I had to be physically lifted from the floor. I wondered what more could happen. My return home would tell.

We arrived back in Wilmore sometime after midnight. Marilyn and I went downstairs to the family room so that I could share with her about the weekend. I had been talking with her by phone during the week to keep her updated on everything that was going on. She informed me that she had told our daughter Candi that "Dad had a vision and you were in it."

Candi had just completed her sophomore year at Asbury College and lived in an apartment under the bedroom wing of our home. I heard music and laughter from her apartment, so I called Candi to greet her and tell her I was home.

"I want to hear the vision you had, and I want to hear it now," she said.

"Can't it wait until tomorrow?" I replied. "It's really long and involved, and if we do it when the rest of the family is awake, I won't have to repeat the story."

"I'm coming over now," Candi insisted. She hung up the phone and in moments was sitting on the other couch in the family room. When I started to share the story of the vision, tears began to fill her eyes.

Candi had been our compliant child until she was fourteen and we moved to Germany. It was an especially hard move for her. The five years in New Jersey had caused her to sink deep roots, and there was much tearing in her spirit during the dislocation of the move. She had also been wounded in love, and her heart seemed encrusted with scar tissue. Our child who had been compliant for years had become distant, hard, and aloof.

Then I began to share with her about the flames in the yard and children dancing in the fire: "Candi, *you* were leading the dance." Suddenly the dam burst and years of hurt, anger, and willful defiance were washed away. She was sobbing uncontrollably as the Holy Spirit began breaking the encrustation that had grown into a hard thickened shell. Candi was being set free to lead the dance.

I held her tightly and rocked her, praying in the spirit the whole time. "I am so sorry for all the harshness and misunderstanding," I mumbled through my tears. She held me tightly and sobbed all the more. "Please forgive me for cheating you all these years, for not letting you into my inner world, for only letting you see me as father and pastor and chaplain. I never let you see inside, Candi. I felt that there was nothing there to give." We both sobbed.

My mind flooded with memories of how controlling and egocentric I had been with the family. Marilyn and I had done all the "right" things with the kids: We gave them our time, memorized Bible verses together, led them to the Lord, taught them manners, monitored their TV watching. But I hovered over them like a hawk watching for any signs of moral failure. I scrutinized their friends, governed their dress, and generally controlled as much of their lives as possible because I was afraid that if I didn't, they might make the same mistakes that I made. I was, in essence, trying to be the Holy Spirit for my family.

"I am so sorry, baby. Will you forgive me?" Breaking was almost complete. "Would you like to ask Jesus to baptize you in His Spirit, to fill the empty and broken places, to love you from the inside out?" I asked. She nodded yes, then began with convulsive breaths to pray, "Lord Jesus, please baptize me in Your Holy Spirit." Her hands raised. She received the promise. She entered the dance. The vision was being fulfilled.

I had Marilyn tell the family that we would get together the next evening for group sharing. I looked forward to relating the week that had just passed. Fifteen people were in the family room as I began to share: My wife, my sister-in-law, a young woman who was an unwed mother, my nephew, my parents-in-law, my children, and five college students (three of whom lived with us). I began again with repentance and confession for cheating the family by not sharing my interior world. I held nothing back. I shared about my deliverance from pornography and masturbation and how, in my fear for them, I tried to do what God alone was supposed to do. Tears began to flow among us all as the Holy Spirit began His work of restoration. I recalled for them the events of the week, the visions, and the prophesy. God broke in.

A phone call came for my sister-in-law, forcing her to leave in order to pick up a family member from work. I asked her if I could pray for her first. She stood in front of me, I held my hands over her head, and I began to pray. She dropped to the floor as if someone had shot her. Her wailing cry pierced the night as she rolled on the floor. The Spirit was performing soul surgery releasing years of pent-up emotion from a difficult relationship and unresolved grief over family issues.

My seventy-seven-year-old mother-in-law rose from the couch and asked me to pray for her. "I need God to set me free," she said. As I extended my hands to her in prayer, she also fell under the power of God and began to cry.

These were people that knew me all too well. I was not to them a prophet with a portfolio. This for me is all the more amazing. My failures, relational shortcomings, and personality quirks had been there for them to see. Yet God in His sovereignty continued to overpower us all.

God moved upon my teenage children. My younger daughter Elizabeth confessed her self-hatred and fear and was healed. We dealt with the rejection she had felt from me all her life. I cradled her in my arms and gave her the Father's and my blessing. Harrison, my fifteen-year-old son, confessed dabbling in alcohol, tobacco, and drugs and prayed in repentance for forgiveness and the healing power of the Spirit's baptism. We were dancing in the fire.

My older daughter, Candi, came forward and brought her brother and sister together, held them, and offered healing prayer for them. She took spiritual authority over the forces that were waging war against them. She was leading the children as they were dancing in the fire. *The vision, O God, the vision. It is truly from You.*

The young woman was slain in the Spirit and received a deep healing and release from the bondage of her unwed pregnancy. While in St. Louis I had seen her too dancing in the fire. Two college students were slain in the Spirit and received special words from the Lord. They began dancing in the fire.

Fall, fire, fall. We are dancing.

I then moved to the others. I prayed for Chad, Shawn, Marilinda, and then Marlene. With each prayer was a growing sense that the Lord Jesus Himself was actively interceding for those over whom I prayed. As I began to pray for Marlene, I was filled with an extraordinary sensing that the Holy Spirit was shifting into overdrive, that something powerful was about to be orchestrated by the Spirit himself. Little was I to know the depth of the miracle that our Lord was about to perform. I had no clue of the nature, severity, or trauma that was about to be healed as Marlene lay on our family room floor. It took a week before Marlene could share with us the mighty miracle that Father accomplished in her life.

Here it is in her own words:

I am Marlene Stokely. I came to Asbury College to start my life over and to seek God's will. A little over two years ago, I went through a very painful divorce. I felt like God had ordained my marriage, that He had given us a ministry and that we were supposed to enter the mission field to work with youth. However, the devil placed a lie between Robin and myself, driving us apart. I think he sent demons of doubt to torment Robin, and slowly managed to devour our home. What began through doubt and deception ended with drugs and unfaithfulness. I think it would have been easier to lose Robin to death than to lose him to satan.

The complete emptiness that I felt after the divorce made me face an unpleasant issue in my life. I had been sexually abused from the time I was a small child until I was about twelve. My abuser, a step-grandfather, told me that my mommy would cry if I told and that it would be my fault. Making Mommy cry is a big deal to a young child, so I remained quiet and stayed chaffed and raw. My mother questioned me. She asked if anyone had been touching me. I wanted to tell her so badly. But I thought that she would cry, so I just lied and said no. She would tell me that Jesus didn't like us to tell stories and that it would make Him unhappy. But I continued to protect my mother from hurt and chose to lie—I had the choice of making my mommy cry or disappointing Jesus. I chose the latter.

All my life I grew up feeling that Jesus was mad at me and that I was a bad person. I strove to be the perfect child, trying to please everyone. I felt so badly about myself that I thought the praise of people would prove to God and to myself that I was a good person. But down deep inside I hated myself.

There were times when I would just lie there and count ceiling tiles while my abuser violated me. I grasped for anything to take my mind off of what was going on. How I loathed myself and everything I felt! How could he hurt me so? Sometimes I would get in the shower and turn the hot water on full-blast, trying to scald off the nastiness. If I could just wash the grime away, perhaps I would quit feeling so empty, hollow, and dirty inside. But nothing ever helped. All my life I felt that something was missing, and that if people really knew me for what I was, they would not love me. This hidden inward hate and the desire to please people—to prove my self-worth—continued to be a very big part of my life until last week.

Two weeks ago I had a dream. I dreamed that I was in an evil place and surrounded by trees—all stripped of their bark, dry, and dead. In the middle of this place stood a huge snake, colored a red that I had never seen before. Yet the snake was transparent as well.

It wrapped itself around me until I could not move. Suddenly I started quoting scriptures—scriptures that I did not remember having memorized. It was as though the Spirit of God was allowing me to recall these scriptures. The snake unwound itself from around me and I woke up. I was sweating and scared. I knew that the snake had been satan. The next day I told my friend Marilinda, who also felt like this dream was from the devil.

I continued to dream about this snake every night for several nights in a row. The devil would bring all sorts of thoughts to my mind each night before I went to sleep. He reminded me of every horrible thing that I had done. He told me that it was my fault that my marriage had ended. Every way that I ever failed my husband came to mind. I was told that the sexual abuse was also my fault—that I could have stopped if I had really wanted it to stop. Crazy stuff filled my mind. I couldn't sleep for all the memories of failure running rapidly through my head. I couldn't even pray. I felt totally worthless and I hated myself like never before.

On Monday, May 21, Dr. Brown invited those of us who lived in his home (three of us college girls live there) to meet in the family room for a time of sharing. We sat among his family and some other college friends as he told us what God had been doing in his life and how the Lord had touched him supernaturally. As he was giving his testimony, I was powerfully touched by what he was saying. Then he prayed for his sister-in-law and she fell slain in the Spirit. As she fell upon the floor, she cried out to God in a wailing-like sound and I knew that God was delivering her from something.

As Dr. Brown continued to pray for the members of his family, one by one they fell under the power of the Spirit of God. Then Dr. Brown prayed for me. He lifted his hands over my head, not touching me, and began to pray. I felt a pressure on the top of my head like someone was pressing down on it, but no one at all was touching me. Then my lower jaw went numb, then my tongue. The sensation went down my left arm and on to my feet, leaving numbness as it went. I found myself falling to the floor and crying out to God in almost a scream.

I instantly felt freedom inside of me—a freedom that I had never experienced before. It was as if the devil had my mind bound and God had reached in and touched it, releasing me from all the confusion that had been tormenting me. It was like God reached down inside of me and ripped out by the roots all the pain and hurt and fear that had been placed inside me as a child. The emptiness that had always resided inside of me was suddenly gone. I lay on the floor unable to move, resting in the Spirit of God. I was finally a whole person. The Lord healed me in a way that no words can ever adequately explain. I feel like I have taken a bath in the precious healing blood of Jesus, totally cleansed and totally whole. And I'm completely free because I've been dancing in the fire.

But God's work among us for the evening was not yet complete. At last, I prayed for my wife Marilyn. She was the one who most knew the glaring inconsistencies—the gaps between my public and private personae. She was the one who for so many years served as a buffer between my strictness and the family. But what a holy time Father gave us. I held my hands outstretched over her head. She fell back into the arms of one of the young men in the room. The Holy Spirit overwhelmed her. He overwhelmed me. God, what a fire! God, what a dance!

9

Telling All the World

Jesus is more concerned with redeeming the world than with preserving a good reputation. (Oswald Chambers)

Tuesday morning came much too early. It was 3:45 a.m. by the time we had finished dancing in the fire in our family room. The college vice-president was standing in my office when I arrived for work around 10:30 a.m. "So glad that you could join us today. I was hoping to see you before I left town." I wasn't completely convinced that his smile was genuine, but it really didn't matter. I still felt slightly drunk from all of the heady Spirit wine from the night before. I smiled back.

I had come to love David Lalka and his wife Ruth since arriving at the college. His temperament and style reminded me of an old next door neighbor and colleague from Army days, making it easy for me to understand him and adapt to his supervision. I was able to connect with him both personally and professionally. "Can you take a few minutes to visit?" I asked. "There's something I need to share with you."

I closed the door and put down my briefcase as David slipped into the chair by the credenza. "I'm sorry that I'm so late," I said, "but I'm glad you're here first thing. We had such a night last night that I was up until almost 4 a.m...."

"Almost 4 a.m.?" he replied incredulously. "Why that late?"

"The Lord came and visited us on Maxey Street last night." I paused to see his response, then continued. "We began shortly after 7 p.m. and continued until the wee hours. The Holy Spirit fell upon us as I was sharing about my trip to St. Louis."

I was interested in gauging David's reaction. A friend had told me once that David was antagonistic toward renewal in the "Toronto Blessing" form. But he had never said or done anything that would indicate his position one way or another.

"Tell me more," he said.

I revealed the events leading up to and including the St. Louis trip, then shared details of what God had done among my family the last two nights. I wept as I shared the freedom that Christ had brought me. Tears brimmed David's eyes.

We sat quietly for a few moments, then David was the first to speak. "Harvey, I believe God brought you to Asbury College to heal the hurts of the last twenty years, but especially the last five." He looked me straight in the eye. "You are extremely blessed." And with these words, he stood and hugged me, then turned to leave. "We'll talk more when I get back to town."

I pondered for a long while what David might have meant by those words. I sensed that he was referring to some lingering institutional pain experienced by the college from leadership transition: Some difficult presidential changes in years past had surfaced as points of discussion in both formal and informal gatherings. But although I didn't fully understand David's words, I thought that there was a prophetic tone to what he was saying.

I scheduled an appointment with Asbury president Dr. David Gyertson for the next morning. I felt strongly about his knowing what had happened in my life. After all, he was the boss—the campus commander—and a good soldier always kept his commander informed. No leader should ever be blindsided by someone raising an issue, either good or bad, that the leader could have known about in advance. I would rather initiate the conversation than one day have the boss call me across the hall and ask why he didn't know something related to one of his key officers. I also looked forward to having an opportunity to praise God for setting me free.

When we met I repeated my full story with nothing withheld. When I finished, he asked me why I was telling him this.

"There are really three reasons," I responded. I described the military model of keeping the commander informed. "I'm sure that you would hear about it sooner or later, and I wanted you to hear it accurately from me. Secondly, I felt that you could understand and identify with the miraculous element of my testimony."

It certainly seemed logical that he could. David Gyertson had come to Asbury from the presidency of Regent University in Virginia Beach, Pat Robertson's graduate school. He had been guest host for the 700 Club and frequently was featured in various media. He had a close affinity with and understanding of the charismatic movement. I was sure he had heard of other mystical encounters similar to mine.

Then I shared the third reason. I valued his opinion. David Gyertson was a man of true wisdom and experience. He sat back and thought a while before responding.

"I have some real trouble with much of what I hear about 'Toronto,' but I have no doubts about the power and validity of your experience. God has done a notable miracle. What you are describing to me sounds like a classical experience of sanctification. But you need to understand," and now there was a strong note of caution in his voice, "not everyone will be nearly as excited about this as you are."

I would discover before the year was up how true this statement was.

* * * *

The jangling of the phone awakened me from a deep and restful sleep. I looked at the alarm clock: it was 6:55 a.m.. Who would be calling at this time on Sunday morning? I tried to sound as if I were awake.

It was Rich Stephenson, my pastor. I had met Rich shortly after coming to Wilmore and had come to love and appreciate him in a special way. In some respects, it had been difficult transitioning from being in the pulpit every Sunday to sitting in the congregation, but Rich's consistently superb preaching ministered to me week after week. I wasn't the only person who recognized his giftedness. Leighton Ford had invited Rich to participate in his Advanced Arrow Leadership Program, a multi-year mentoring opportunity designed to enhance and support fifteen leaders of innovative churches from around the nation.

"Harvey, sorry to call so early on Sunday, but when I got into town last night, there was an urgent note from Mark. Said something about a power encounter you had with the Holy Spirit in St. Louis—that perhaps I should consider having you speak and tell about it in church this morning."

Rich had just returned from preaching in another state that week. His associate, Mark Nysewander, was present at our Wednesday morning men's prayer meeting when I shared what the Lord had done in my life.

He continued, "I've been praying about this since 5 a.m. this morning and just can't shake it. I believe that the Lord wants you to share what happened."

"Do you know any of the details, Rich?"

"No. Mark just wrote that it was the most powerful thing he had heard in years."

"I've got something you need to read before I say yes. Are you at the office?"

I thought that he needed to know exactly what I would share. Our young church was very contemporary and cutting-edge in worship style, and although in ignorance some of the town old-timers thought we were a charismatic or "Toronto" church, we were really quite traditional theologically. I had never seen any kind of physical manifestation during worship, although I knew that some persons in the congregation had experienced some form of renewal. My perception was that most were just radically committed to our mission statement: reaching the world for Christ through a new generation.

I dressed and drove to the church offices in about ten minutes. In my hand was a computer printout of an e-mail message that I had sent to Randy Clark. He had requested an account of my St. Louis experience so that he might share it while speaking in England that week. When I walked into Rich's office, I handed him the document.

"This is ten pages long!" he said, astonished.

"Well, a lot happened to me," I replied.

When Rich finished reading, he looked up. "I see what you mean. This is going to stretch a lot of people."

"Rich, I'll consent to sharing only if you gather the leadership team together, have them read my testimony, and they concur unanimously that I should speak. If there is not complete agreement, I won't."

He agreed to assemble the leadership during the first part of worship and distribute a photocopy of my testimony to each person. They would read it, pray together and then decide. I was told that I would know their decision shortly after the offering.

Rich came up to me during a fellowship break following the morning offering. "You're on, brother." So I was.

After some introductory remarks outlining Mark's note and our conversations of the morning, my pastor urged the congregation to give a prayerful hearing to what I would share. He then turned the microphone over to me.

I told the whole story, complete with tears. I had just learned the night before about Marlene's deliverance, so I had invited her to share as well. After we had both finished I gave an invitation. The altar filled with people. Many were set free and healed that morning. There were also some manifestations of the Spirit's presence, including some folks falling to the floor when prayed for.

Word quickly spread among the college-aged kids in town that the Lord God had made a house call on Maxey Street. Even though spring semester had ended two weeks before, a number of college-aged kids still lived in Wilmore, many either children of college or seminary employees or "townies"—kids who lived here but whose families had no formal relationship with either institution. They just started showing up at the house Wednesday evening.

Before we knew it, we had a basement of young people sitting and talking about everything that God was doing. I shared the events that had transpired in my own life recently, and told them that I believed that Father wanted to minister in power to those who would receive His work in their lives. I also told them that I was convinced that part of what God was doing in the earth was calling His Bride to holiness. After sharing an informal teaching from the scriptures, I asked if anyone wanted to receive prayer ministry. A number nodded they did.

I began to pray for individuals as they indicated that they wanted prayer. One young man named Dwight came and stood before me. As I prayed, he collapsed to the floor, but something about this was different from other collapses. He started writhing on the carpet, making deep guttural noises, and foaming at the mouth. Demons were manifesting themselves through him.

We gathered around and took authority over the unclean spirits in his life. As we continued, the Holy Spirit began to operate the gift of discernment. As I rebuked each spirit by name, we entered into "hand-to-hand" spiritual warfare. The demons shook him. Bodily fluids flowed from his nose and mouth as he wretched and gagged.

When the demons finally realized that I knew the authority of the Word in the power of the Holy Spirit, they came out whimpering like whipped puppies. Dwight lay motionless and exhausted on the floor as a spirit of praise filled our family room. Glory to Him who sits on the throne!

On another night, a young woman knocked on our door. I had met her earlier in the year at the college and had seen her most recently on the night of Dwight's deliverance. Her father was a professor in our town. "Are you all having a meeting here tonight?" she asked shyly.

"No, but come in," said Marilyn. We offered Wendy[1] a seat.

She sat down nervously. "I'm glad that no one's here. I prayed that the Lord would let me be with you all by myself tonight."

I glanced at Marilyn, then back to Wendy. "So there are some things that you wanted to talk about privately with us."

Tears started rolling softly down her cheeks. "I heard you when you spoke in church, and then I saw what the Lord did here last week. I knew that I needed to talk with you and get your help." Wendy revealed a story of a brokenhearted little girl who never felt that she received love and acceptance from her father. Although it was her story, I knew that it was the story of so many kids in clergy families. It had been the story of my own children—at least, until St. Louis.

She talked about an emotionally distant, perfectionist father who was continually winning the world for Jesus but at home was distant, aloof, and unapproachable. She described times that they wanted Dad's attention, but he would plop down in front of the television and tune them out. She wept harder as she shared the deep pain of her rejection. "I keep thinking that God must be like Daddy. I don't feel that I can ever please Him. No matter how hard I try I always know that I can never measure up to His expectations." My heart broke as I listened to Wendy's pain and rejection. I grieved over how her father's attitudes and behavior were blocking her from being able to receive and understand her heavenly Father's love.

---

1. Name has been changed.

Wendy agreed to let Marilyn and me pray for her. As we began, her soft crying turned into convulsive sobs. Marilyn prayed softly in the Spirit while I spoke to this hurting child. "I want to stand here in the place of your father, Wendy. For the next few minutes I want to represent him in what's called identificational repentance." I then prayed and, on behalf of her father, repented before her and asked her forgiveness. I imparted the Fathers' blessing to her. The look of God's peace and love came upon her face as she let her heavenly Father wrap His arms around her. She fell into my arms, and I gently eased her to the floor as the Holy Spirit continued to soak her in His wonderful love and mercy.

* * * *

On Friday afternoon, I left the office early to begin a two-week road trip representing Asbury College to some major donors and speaking before different groups in Georgia and the Carolinas. I always enjoyed the opportunities I had to speak when traveling, and especially this trip. Not only would I get to preach in my childhood church and see my parents, I was going to speak in a Southern Baptist Church that was experiencing renewal. However, before I could leave, I had to complete a number of details such as stopping by the bank, picking up shirts from the laundry, paying a few bills, and getting the oil changed in the car.

These routine tasks ended up being anything but routine.

The dry cleaners and laundry was the first business establishment in Wilmore's little block-long town business district. I pulled up in my car and ran into retrieve my dress shirts. As I waited for Carolyn (the lady at the counter) to get my change, a sudden sneeze suprised me. I turned away in order to retrieve my handkerchief. When I faced the counter again, Carloyn was standing there with my change in her hand—and tears running down her cheeks.

"Is everything OK?" It felt like a stupid question, but that's all that came out of my mouth at the moment.

"I just have to have Jesus in my life," she replied.

Wow, I thought, *God is here. Why would she be telling me this if the Holy Spirit were not prompting her?* Carolyn didn't know that I was a preacher, she only knew me as "Mr. Brown—heavy starch." Yet here she was pleading with me to lead her to the Savior.

My first impulse normally might have been to say "I'll pray for you" or invite her to church, but I sensed that God wanted to meet her right then, right there. I had seen Him reveal His heart so powerfully in the last two weeks, why not right here on Main Street? The fire in the vision had not only been at my house and the college, but had also rolled through the center of town.

"Carolyn, Jesus is here and wants more than anything to be a part of your life. I'd love to pray with you and for you right now. Is that okay?"

"Oh Mr. Brown, I want to so much. But I've done all this horrible stuff in my life, I don't know if it would do any good."

"Believe me, it will. May I pray with you?"

She nodded, and I stepped to the end of the counter where I could comfortably take her hand while we prayed. As soon as I touched her, she staggered as if she were about to fall.

What do I do, Lord? She's about to go down under the power of the anointing of your presence. I'm the only one here. What would it look like if somebody came in and saw me standing over the laundry lady's body? Couldn't you have a sister in the Lord come by to help with this ministry? I was really apprehensive about the issue of my being a man involved in solo ministry like this with a woman.

Just then, Carolyn said "Look! There's Jeana. She's been talking to me about the Lord."

I turned and looked through the store window. On the other side of the street was a young woman who I had never seen before. I stuck my head out the door and called, "Jeana!" When she entered the laundry, I explained what had just happened and told her about my unspoken prayer asking the Lord for a sister to help in ministering to Carolyn.

"I was just prayer-walking Main Street," Jeana exclaimed, "and was praying specifically for Carolyn's salvation! This is an answer to prayers I've prayed for a long, long time." And her appearance was certainly an answer to my prayer of just moments before.

When we began to pray for Carolyn she doubled over in a crunch-like motion. Her eyes rolled back in their sockets then rebounded into focus as she looked at me wildly. A chill went down my spine. This was warfare.

"In the mighty, powerful, and victorious Name of Jesus…" I confronted the darkness that was controlling Carolyn. For the next hour and a half, Jeana and I, like a small squad of freedom fighters, engaged the enemy on Carolyn's behalf. With it being Friday afternoon, believing customers would enter the laundry like reinforcements, joining our prayer. Others would step inside, see what was happening, then turn and leave. One college administrator's wife came in, took one look, and slowly backed out the door.

At one time more than half a dozen people were praying and interceding for Carolyn as we ministered to her. Even my secretary and her college-aged son, coming to pick up laundry, ended up as part of the circle. This deliverance was becoming like a bizarre video game in which we found ourselves moving through a series of spiritual doors pursuing the master of Carolyn's stronghold. We fought through layer after layer of hurt, wounding, rejection, and sin until we sensed that we were finally assaulting the enemy's headquarters.

Through the blood of Jesus and the power of His Word, the enemy's grip was broken and he was routed. I began to pray for an infilling of the presence of the Spirit of God when Carolyn cried, "I see fire, I see fire! Oh, I feel the fire! Glory to God, I feel the fire!" She collapsed to the floor and lay motionless, her distress replaced by a visible serenity.

* * * *

I was surprised by how young and energetic Gary Folds' voice sounded over the phone. He was pastor of Second Baptist Church in my hometown of Macon, Georgia. Although I was familiar with this large Southern Baptist congregation, I would have never thought to make contact with the pastor had not Carol and John Arnott suggested it. They knew Gary because of the powerful touch he had received through renewal. I had decided to call him and introduce myself since I was going to Macon to address an Asbury alumni gathering at a Methodist meeting. During our conversation he invited me to speak at Second Baptist for Saturday Night Life, a weekly renewal gathering.

In St. Louis, Jack Taylor had held up a copy of *Bull in a China Shop*, Gary Folds' book, and declared that his friend Gary was the surest indication that the current renewal was valid. Gary had been an ultra-Baptist—a fundamentalist, cessationist, separatist—who, when powerfully touched by the Holy Spirit, entered into a new Spirit-led walk with Christ. Gary had migrated overnight from being Mr. Baptist to being a believer who with childlike simplicity daily trusted Father to teach him His ways. I looked forward to meeting him in person, as well as being in fellowship with brothers and sisters who were experiencing renewal. It was like I would get to walk in two different worlds on the same trip: my "college" world, and the newly discovered "renewal" world.

On my first full day in Georgia I was scheduled to play golf with a wealthy philanthropist patron of the college. Since I was a United Methodist clergyman, he arranged for Dr. John Horton, the local United Methodist district superintendent, to join us as our fourth player. Dr. Horton offered me a ride, and after we had gone only two blocks, he asked me, "How did you get invited to speak at Second Baptist Church on Saturday night?"

I was stunned. How did he, the Methodist district superintendent, know that I was going to be speaking at a renewal service? The invitation had come only three days before.

"Well, I guess my cover as a mild-mannered Methodist preacher has been blown," I jested.

"It sure has. My secretary attends Second Baptist and was excited that you were going to be speaking. I'd be there to hear you if Linda and I hadn't planned an anniversary getaway to the beach. But back to my original question," he smiled. "Why are you speaking there?"

It was plain to see that John wasn't being antagonistic but simply curious. I explained how the Arnotts had connected me with Gary, then retraced the steps leading to my personal renewal and dancing in the fire. We arrived at the golf course before I had finished my story, but John was so intrigued that he kept circling the block until I was through.

* * * *

When Gary Folds and I entered the sanctuary of Second Baptist Church at 7 p.m. on Saturday, it was already full, and chairs had been placed in the aisles. Soon even the extra seats were filled, and latecomers began to line the walls. Who would have ever thought that you would find standing-room-only crowds at a Baptist Church on a Saturday night? By the time I went to the platform to speak, the building was packed.

I shared my story about the powerful deliverance that Father had brought me and the healing that He was working within my family. When I finished, I invited those who wanted to be free from sexual bondage to come forward for prayer. The ministry team began to pray with the huge number of people, both men and women, who responded. Others gathered around me desiring that I pray with them.

I had never seen a response like this in all my years of preaching. People continually streamed down the aisles. The presence of the Holy Spirit was powerfully evident, and ministry continued until almost one in the morning. Many tearful folk sought a release that previous to my sharing they felt they had no hope in attaining. Men who identified themselves as ministers and church leaders came forward. Others shared the pain of sexual abuse by family members, or came to experience a fresh touch from God. With each prayer, I sensed the compassion of the Father's heart for His kids—these people. And I wanted more than anything to be a vehicle of His blessing for them.

The next morning I preached a sermon entitled "As It Was in the Days of Noah" at my childhood church, Cherokee Heights United Methodist. When I gave a call to accept Christ, four people responded. After we prayed to invite Jesus Christ in their lives, I challenged them to come forward and make their commitments public. One was an elderly usher who served on the church's Administrative Board.

On Monday, as I left town, I stopped by Second Baptist to visit with Gary and pray. When I left he handed me an audiocassette. "Here's a tape of Saturday night's service. I thought you might like to have it." I figured I would listen to it on the road.

My destination was Hilton Head, South Carolina, and a meeting with a former president of Columbia. The monotonous rows of slash pine on Interstate 16 began to lull me into sleepiness as I cruised down that barren and lonely stretch of concrete. Reaching for the audiocassette, I popped it into the rental car's stereo and was quickly enlivened by the worship. I heard Gary Folds introduce me, and as my speaking began I experienced something I had never known before. It wasn't unusual for me to review tapes of my sermons and critique myself. But what was unusual was the physical sensations I began to experience in the car as I listened to the message. I found myself powerfully touched and I started to cry. Then what felt like waves of God's glory began to go up and down through my chest cavity and I entered into a spirit of praise and rejoicing. I had heard of anointing during preaching before, but never had I felt such anointing and unction of the Holy Spirit. I was getting blasted while listening to my own voice. Before I realized it, I had closed my eyes and lifted my hands toward heaven.

The thump-thump-thumping of the tires on the grass startled me back into present reality. I had run off the road and was going sixty-five miles an hour in the median. I managed to get the car under control and pulled off to the side of the road giggling uncontrollably, not sure whether I was experiencing holy laughter or gross embarrassment. Nonetheless, I sat there until I had regained my composure and my lightheadedness had left. Only then did I think it was safe to operate the car...without the tape playing. I could hardly image what it would have been like trying to explain to a state trooper why I had been driving like a drunk man.

10

No Reserve, No Retreat, No Regret

Revival begins when Christians stop talking about other people's sins and start confessing their own. (Corrie ten Boom)

The little coffee shop buzzed with conversation as old friends greeted one another and swapped stories. These informal conference breaks were just as important as the business sessions taking place in the nearby auditorium. Our annual denominational meeting served as much to maintain relationships with the brethren as it did to conduct church business.

I had just sat down with Dr. Kenneth Lloyd Sprinkle, a United Methodist pastor from the Chattanooga area. Ken and I had been friends since the mid-seventies, when we pastored in adjacent towns in Virginia. Having maintained contact with him periodically over the years, I valued him as a friend and a brother. When I asked him how things in his church were going, Ken shared a dynamic shift in terms of how he did ministry. He excitedly described a renewed faith in the Holy Spirit's power to actively work through him as he ministered to his congregation. I was all ears.

I had admired Ken for a number of reasons, not the least of which was his keen intellect. He was plainly one of the most intelligent men that I knew. This was balanced, however, by a child-like simplicity to trust God and serve Him with deep and genuine humility. I had observed Ken laboring faithfully for years in small rural parishes, where he poured out his life for the brothers and sisters in the faith. Now he was pastoring a sizable church serving a growing community on the southern edge of the city.

He had attended some recent renewal meetings in Knoxville, Tennessee, where Randy Clark had been speaking and—much like me—had been powerfully touched by the Lord's work. As a result, he had taken some new steps of faith in praying for people's healing and integrating spiritual gifts into the regular life of his church. He had also sensed that conditions were right to introduce the congregation to more of the renewal work the Holy Spirit seemed to be doing worldwide.

We excitedly talked about Ken hosting a five-day renewal conference at his church in the fall. Since there had already been little outbreaks of the Spirit's presence there, Ken dubbed the conference "Fanning the Flame." After I mentioned that Gary Shelton had suggested leading worship sometime when I spoke, Ken and I decided to see if Gary could assemble a worship team for the conference. The longer we shared, the more it seemed that the Holy Spirit was orchestrating a divine rendezvous: My emerging ministry of renewal was about to have its debut in a mainline church.

I had spent much time reflecting on my experiences in St. Louis and everything that had happened since. I had no doubt that God had performed a powerful miracle within me. I was also convinced, because of the strong prophetic word I had received, that He was commissioning me to proclaim in its fullness the message of the sanctifying fire of the Holy Spirit. Demonstrations of power would accompany the message and the impartation of holiness. For too long God's people had pursued power encounters without first pursuing holiness. It was clear to me now that Father was cleansing the bride, making her fit for the revelation of His Son the Groom. I needed to plainly declare the truth of God's power, not just to forgive and heal but to keep us continually clean in the holiness, mercy, and grace of Father's love.

Preparations for the meetings began in earnest as Ken and his church members developed the idea of "Fanning the Flame." Volunteers ensured that every detail was carefully planned and prayed for. Special periods of prayer and fasting were declared, and many participated in marshaling all available spiritual and temporal resources for the meetings. Ken also conducted special ministry-team training to equip a group of mature believers for providing prayer ministry for seekers at the conference.

At the same time, Gary Shelton was assembling a superb team of worship musicians who would lead us in corporate praise and worship. Ken printed and distributed copies of my testimony within the church and among area clergy who were invited to participate. He also arranged a local pastors' luncheon in conjunction with the meetings, where clergy could discuss God's current move. Another preparation was occurring, though, that was completely spontaneous and sovereign: Father was raising a small army of prayer warriors worldwide who were committed to lifting me up in prayer.

One thing spoken prophetically over me by Jim Goll—almost like an aside or afterthought—was "Now, that man is probably going to need some intercessors." He had then prayed, "Okay, Lord, I ask that You raise up intercessors." I was fascinated by how Father managed to do that, and some of the surprises that came as a result.

One day when I opened my mail, I found a prayer covenant signed by forty-five people from Livingston, Tennessee. After they learned of my ministry through their Bible study leader, they were led by the Holy Spirit to commit themselves to regular and faithful prayer for me. As a sign of their seriousness to being intercessors, they had fashioned and signed a covenant. Other ministries like Sister Gwen Shaw and the End Times Handmaidens "took me on" as a regular prayer concern. On one occasion, I was walking through the hotel lobby during a national renewal conference when I said hello to a group of ladies. One of them called after me: "Wait a minute! I just saw your name tag. You're Harvey Brown, and I've been praying for you!" She then shared with me how a friend had told her of my ministry and she too had felt a divine calling to become one of my intercessors.

By the time "Fanning the Flame" arrived, it seemed that all involved had done everything possible to effectively prepare for the event. Publicity was pervasive, prayer was persistent, and praise was coming. Gary had assembled a terrific musical team: Jeff James on bass, Mike McClung on drums, and James Dillingham (Wayne Watson's guitarist) on lead guitar. They would be augmented by other musicians and singers from Ken's church. Gary was a concerned, however, over how "Vineyard-style" music and worship would be received in a denominational church, and revealed that he was a little uptight since he had never ministered in a mainline church before. Ken reassured him that anointed praise and worship—no matter what style—would be welcomed.

He was absolutely right.

In a somewhat unusual arrangement, the meetings began on Saturday night. Worship seemed rather subdued, but I told myself that it was the first night and we were just "checking each other out." When I opened the altar for people to come forward, I was surprised by the large number of respondents. The ministry team fanned out in pairs and prayed with individuals as Gary and the worship team played. One brother from the ministry team had been assigned as my partner through the evening to assist me as I prayed for people.

The first persons to come to me to receive prayer were a mother with two young daughters who appeared to be four and seven. I stepped down to floor-level to be closer to them. Although the mother said that the little girls had asked to come forward, I wasn't sure whether it was their idea or hers. Still, I wanted to be approachable.

I knelt on the floor, looking eye-to-eye with the girls, and introduced myself as Harvey. The youngest clung to her mother's leg, and when I asked her if she wanted me to talk to Jesus for her, she shook her head no and buried her face in her mother' skirt. "That's alright," I said, "I don't have to pray if you don't want me to." I was trying to sound like TV's Mr. Rogers, but I wasn't sure that it was working. "Jesus loves you soooo much, and He thinks that you are very, very special." The girl stole a glance, then quickly hid her face again. I patted her shoulder, then turned to the older sister. Perhaps she would be easier to deal with. But as I started to talk, she burst into tears. *Oh boy,* I thought. *How in the world do I deal with this?*

"What's your name?" I asked, hoping Mr. Rogers would work better this time, but she cried all the harder. Inwardly I was uttering a frantic prayer, hoping that the Lord would show me how to redeem the situation. *Ask her if she wants to ask Jesus into her heart,* said an inner voice that I recognized as the Holy Spirit. *She is old enough to follow me. Her crying is conviction of sin. Go ahead and ask her now.*

As kindly as possible, I told the older girl how much Jesus loved her and that He wanted to forgive her sins and come into her life. When I asked if she wanted to have Jesus in her heart, she nodded yes. I explained that all she had to do was ask Him, and that I would pray for her. I reached out to place my hand on her head to pray when suddenly she fell forward into my arms. She was gone—completely out in the Spirit. I gently laid her on the lower level of the platform where, for the next two hours, she lay motionless with the exception of a twitching right arm. I wept as I saw her resting in the Lord. Her actions were completely unrehearsed and unprompted. There was no auto-suggestion because she was the first person that I had prayed for, and she had not previously seen the phenomenon. I could only imagine the spiritual communion she was having with the Lord while she lay on the floor. God was here, and He was here in power. I quickly handed this up to Him for His glory.

* * * *

The two morning services went well, although attended almost exclusively by members of Ken's church. Sunday night's service was the first that gained the feel of a renewal meeting. From the moment that

Gary and the team began to play, I definitely sensed that the night would be special.

When the time arrived, Ken announced that we would take two forms of offering. We would first give an offering of praise to the Lord, with two or three people sharing what God had done for them since the conference began. Second, we would take a regular offering in order to pay conference expenses. Testimonies were begun by a lady from the back of the church, and one by one others began to share. After a few testimonies, Ken tried to return to the front with the microphone, but each time, someone else wanted to praise God for something they had received. Each testimony was increasingly powerful as brothers and sisters shared the fantastic things that God had done just in the last two days. It reminded me of the continuing narrative in the book of Acts, as believers reported the great things that God had done.

Ken finally realized that we would have only one offering—an offering of praise—and sat down on the platform. Anni Shelton came forward to ask if she could share a word that she felt the Lord was speaking, and her comments were immediately reinforced by another prophetic utterance through Jeff James. As we sat quietly, savoring the Lord's presence and pondering what He was saying to the church, I slipped up to the platform and sat next to Ken.

He leaned over and whispered, "Where do we go from here?"

I whispered back, "I don't know. I thought you were flying this ship!"

All at once it struck me as funny, and I started to chuckle. Before I knew it, I was laughing but trying my best not to let it show. Ken started laughing too because all he wanted to do was take the offering. All God wanted was to be in charge.

About the same time, the congregation burst out laughing as well. We were all suddenly overwhelmed with total and absolute hilarity. I was laughing so hard that my sides felt like they were going to split. Here we were, dignified Doctors Brown and Sprinkle, literally rolling on the floor in the chancel cackling with laughter. Tears ran down our cheeks as we leaned on each other giggling uncontrollably. I looked over to the side and saw Gary Shelton on his hands and knees slapping the floor in delirium. I don't know how long we laughed, but it seemed like an eternity as God allowed us to experience extravagant joy.

Somehow in all this, Gary recovered enough to begin playing "Mercy is Falling." As suddenly as the laughter began, the congregation poured into the aisles and the front of the church and began to dance. Little gray-haired ladies were dancing next to bearded construction workers, children were dancing with parents. I found myself swinging Ken around on my arm square-dance fashion, then being passed off to a huge brother who literally swung me! It was a joyous celebration of God's love as I saw young and old, male and female, rich and poor set aside their hang-ups and inhibitions long enough to give themselves totally to Father in praise. We danced and danced and danced before the Lord.

When the celebration finally died down a little, Ken made an announcement: "For those of you who are guests with us tonight, I ought to let you know that this is not a normal Sunday night service—yet!" At which point the congregation erupted into spontaneous applause and cheering. God had broken up the meeting at the Methodist church.

Monday night's meeting was an entirely different story, however. Worship seemed flat. My message seemed dull and (at least to me) rambling. Nothing seemed to click. There was no fire, no spark. It wasn't until Tuesday night that the Lord revealed the problem.

It had seemed good to Ken and me to have a time of testimony each night so that people could celebrate together the great things that Father was doing in their midst. But while folks were sharing, I was having a grumbling session with the Lord in my spirit. *Why, Lord? Why? You were so real on Sunday night. Have You abandoned us? What did we do?*

Then I heard the clear tones of the Holy Spirit. *It's not what you have done, it's what you haven't done,* He said. *You were victorious Sunday night because you took high ground through prayer and fasting. You were celebrating a battle that had been won above the clouds. But you did not continue to press the battle. Where was your praying on Monday, where was your intercession for the work of My Spirit? You were resting in the memory of yesterday's victory. But like manna, good only for one day, yesterday's victory is sufficient for yesterday alone. You, as a leader of My people, failed them by not seeking Me. Seek Me with all your heart, then you will find Me.*

My heart was beating so fast in my chest that I thought it was going to leap through my shirt. Tears coursed down my cheeks. God was right. But of course He was right. He was God. I had failed to press into the holy place because I was too busy enjoying the memory of Sunday night. Every good soldier knows how important it is to reinforce his foxhole after one battle and prior to the next. Yet I had let down my guard and was enjoying the view from the high ground we had taken rather than strengthening our position through earnest prayer and fasting.

I began to grieve. Ken finally asked if anyone else wanted to share. I stood up and took the microphone. Haltingly, I began to speak. I told the congregation what the Lord had just said to me, then repented before them of my failure in leadership. As I spoke, Anni Shelton got on her face and began to mourn before the Lord. I handed Ken the microphone and prostrated myself. Sobs shook my body as I grieved over my sin and how it had affected the people.

In a matter of moments, Ken was beside me, to repent of his carelessness in prayer since the victory of Sunday night. More and more people began to grieve over their sins and repent in the Spirit's presence. The altar started to fill as the Spirit of Holiness swept back and forth across the congregation. We mourned our sins and grieved for the lost. People were again in the aisles, this time not dancing but mourning. I invited clergy to come forward and receive prayer if they needed it. That evening I saw Baptist,

Methodist, Episcopalian, Presbyterian, and Pentecostal ministers slain in the Spirit. One brother who had been reluctant about all this stuff—a former Marine Corps officer who was now an Episcopal priest—went down like someone had taken a two-by-four and hit him behind the knees.

Around ten that evening, while I was praying for someone, I saw a tall man in his thirties step inside the sanctuary. He stood by the door for a few minutes watching, then approached me when I was available. He was well-dressed, in an olive double-breasted suit, white shirt, and handsome tie. "I was watching you, and the anointing of God is all over you. Would you please pray for me?"

Although I knew that he had not been at the service, I sensed that this was still a divine appointment. I told him that I would pray, and as I extended my hand toward him he immediately fell over backwards. I leaned down, put my hand on his head, and continued to pray for awhile. For an hour after I had moved on, this young man lay motionless on the floor. Later that night, I learned his story as relayed by one of the ushers.

The man was an international evangelist for the Church of God in Cleveland, Tennessee, who had been conducting revival meetings in another part of the city. As he was driving down Battlefield Parkway, the Holy Spirit told him to go to the Methodist church. When he approached the church, he was surprised to find the lights on and the parking lot still full of cars. Not knowing why he was there, he stepped in the door, saw me praying, and heard the Spirit say that he was to have me pray for him. While he was out in the Spirit, he was pleading with Father not to allow the Spirit to depart his denomination. He feared that as a church they had lost their first love and were grieving the Holy Spirit. "How ironic," he said, "that I would be overcome by the Spirit of God and find myself stretched out for an hour on the floor of a Methodist church." God is indeed a God of ironies.

Modern Pentecostalism grew out of a Wesleyan theological base—a theology of a second work of grace known as the baptism in the Holy Spirit. The irony is that, although we Methodists have a cross and flame in our official denominational symbol, we all too rarely encounter the power of either in our churches. We, like the Church of God our brother represented, are no longer movements but institutions. And as institutional theory demonstrates, established structures almost always repel new movements that challenge institutional beliefs or call institutional practice into question. This has been a significant hurdle as renewal moves across the face of the church, not only for churches like Ken Sprinkle's that represent mainline denominations, but even for third-wave churches that have existed long enough to operate with established norms and practices.

Churches who embrace renewal run the risk of allowing God to escape denominationally shaped boxes. The result is not always tidy and is frequently boisterous, and some church members (perhaps occasionally many) find themselves uncomfortable with the new style. They either may go slipping quietly away to another place of worship or leave hollering and screaming about "what somebody has done to our church."

In reality, renewal frequently is blamed for all kinds of discord in the church when, if the facts were fully known, many of these issues were nurtured underground for years, only to be forced to the surface by renewal. I know nothing more effective than genuine renewal for clarifying where we stand in regard to the things of God. As I once heard, God is in the business of offending the mind in order to reveal the condition of the heart.

Dr. Sprinkle's church experienced renewal during the five days of "Fanning the Flame." They also experienced a certain degree of backlash from members who thought that the meetings "weren't Methodist." Some have slipped quietly away, others have gone kicking and screaming wild and unfounded accusations toward the pastor and me. But the reality is, God showed up and met powerfully with us.

You can ask the lady who was suffering from multiple personality disorder and was (according to her therapist) completely "merged" while doing carpet time in the Spirit. Or you could ask the burned-out Baptist missionary who had his wounded spirit healed and his zeal for the Lord restored. Perhaps you should talk to the Christian counselor who, through prayer, was healed of a four-year bout with clinical depression, as well as recovering feeling and movement in the left side of her face twenty years after brain surgery left it paralyzed.

Melissa would tell you how God healed her heart that was broken through divorce and scarred by backsliding. You could listen to the testimony of a man whose physician describes the miracle that cured his diabetes after fifteen years of insulin injections. Or Mike and Karen would tell you that God rekindled their first love, and to this day their lives and family are different. All of these, along with others, have testified that their lives were touched by God and irrevocably changed. They too have been dancing in the fire.

11

In the Shadow of Goliath

Pray continually (1 Thessalonians 5:17).

I felt rather odd sitting alone at the little table in the restaurant. There were twenty-five hundred believers at the meeting, yet I was feeling lonely and isolated. *The seminar sessions are just ending*, I thought. *Maybe there's someone I know in the lobby who I can invite to eat with me.*

I placed the menu on the table and stepped out of the restaurant hoping to find someone I recognized. The lobby was packed with strangers. Feeling somewhat dejected I made my way back to the table. *Traveling is glamorous only to those who don't do it*, I thought to myself.

I noticed a man wearing a clerical collar sitting alone. His name tag suggested he was part of the conference, so I approached him. Reaching out to someone else would the best way to deal with my own sense of isolation—and there was no need for both of us to eat alone. He brightened at my invitation and quickly joined me. Little did I know that this seemingly spontaneous act would have eternal repercussions.

My new friend introduced himself as the Reverend Ken Steigler, pastor of old Wesley United Methodist Church in Salem, Massachusetts. He was a jolly man in his early or mid-fifties whose contagious laugh and twinkling eyes spoke volumes about the joy of the Lord in his life. As we ate, we delightfully shared what God was doing in our respective worlds. I asked Ken about his ministry in Salem. What he unraveled was a twisted tale that resembled a Frank Peretti novel. It startled, shocked, and surprised me.

I knew very little about Salem other than the fact that it was located a few miles north of Boston. I had some impressions of the infamous Salem witch trials of 1692 because of Arthur Miller's play *The Crucible*, but I had no idea of the present habitation of darkness in the city. Ken now told me of the pervasive demonic presence and grip of witchcraft over the area. I sat spellbound as he poured out story after story of God's mercy to him as he labored in a city that sounded more like Ahaz and Jezebel's Samaria than a city bearing the Hebrew name for "peace."

Ken was a Spirit-filled survivor, and his five-year tenure as pastor of Wesley Church made him the longest-lasting Protestant pastor in the city. It seemed that other pastors became physically or psychologically incapacitated, fell into sin and left the area, or died. Ken related the relentless oppression that he and the small community of believing Christians experienced. He continued by describing a town where four major darkness groups were militantly active, witches and warlocks held key posts in every government department, and the last two weeks of each October were given over to "Haunted Happenings"—a city-sponsored festival dedicated to celebrating evil and attracting between 600,000 and 800,000 people.

The more Ken talked, the more my spirit was rising up within me. This pastor and a small contingent of brothers and sisters were fighting hard to hold their ground while standing in the shadow of Goliath, but they desperately needed reinforcements for a breakthrough. I began to feel what David must have felt when he heard the taunts of the huge Philistine toward the armies of Israel. Someone needed to go fight this enemy of the Lord who dared to defy and blaspheme the Holy One of heaven.

As an Army paratrooper, I knew the adrenaline rush of standing in the door of an airplane and preparing to jump with full combat equipment. It was the same sensation I was now feeling as Ken continued. My spirit was gearing up for battle, because soon I was going to be in a spiritual combat free-fire zone: Salem, Massachusetts.

After Ken finished sharing, he asked about me. I explained how the Lord had led me to the administration of Asbury College and about the renewal in my life. Since I had a copy of my e-mail testimony, I asked if he would like to review it after lunch. He poured over the manuscript while his ice cream melted—ignored—in the dessert bowl.

"You have to come to Salem, Harvey," he said finally. "You just have to come. I know it's the Lord, just as surely as I know I'm sitting across this table from you." Ken laughed as he continued in his staccato style New England accent. "This is a marvelous appointment the Lord has for us, isn't it?"

I agreed with Ken and shared what I had been feeling ever since he had begun to speak. After some more talk, he invited me to preach "contra darkness" during the last week of October. His church had already been planning some events in order to reach folks who come to Salem's festival, but now Ken was convinced that the church should expand the vision to include a week of special preaching, culminating in an ecumenical concert of prayer and street witnessing on Halloween.

"I think the time is right for us to press forward in a new way, Harvey. Will you come?"

I agreed that I would.

I was understanding more and more Jim Goll's comment about my needing intercessors. If there were ever a time when I would need prayer covering, this would be it. I mobilized my new prayer network by focusing on the upcoming meetings in Salem. I knew the seriousness of this conflict: We would be assaulting a massive stronghold of darkness. To win the battle would require strategy, training, preparation, and courage. I had no delusions about the situation's seriousness, nor about the Lord's ability to make us mighty enough to pull down strongholds.

The fact that I was a retired soldier wasn't lost on me as I considered all the dynamics of this conflict. My work with combat units over years provided a thorough framework for understanding what an army must do to win a battle. What faced me in Salem was in many ways no different from other kinds of military conflicts. But I had a singular advantage over my adversary: Before the first volley would be fired, I knew what the outcome would be. The battle was already won because of what Jesus accomplished on Calvary.

To train for the battle, I increased my "PT." For a normal soldier, PT stood for "physical training," but for me, as a Christian, it primarily meant "prayer time." I was to the point in my walk where prayer wasn't a luxury or an afterthought, but a vital part of the day so I could center myself in the heart of God. My pre-renewal prayers frequently informed God what I planned to do and asked Him to bless it. Now I was yearning to learn in advance what Father wanted me to do, so that I could align myself with it and walk each step Spirit led.

Part of my training for Salem would occur in St. Louis in early October. Following meetings in Wichita and Tulsa, I went to St. Louis to facilitate a one-day consultation with Randy Clark and part of his staff. I remained as their guest for the "Walking in the Prophetic" conference where I received what I felt was a crash course in listening to the Holy Spirit. Although I had been in ministry for twenty-five years and carried impeccable credentials, in many areas I felt like a rookie—particularly when it came to revelatory gifts. I was hungry to learn everything possible about what God was saying when it came time to minister to individuals.

Gnawing feelings of impotence lingered from earlier ministry years when someone with desperate human need sought my help. Now I was no longer solely dependent upon my own resources for answers. The God of the universe, my Father, loves all His children and desires to speak to them in order to heal them and to reveal His heart.

"Walking in the Prophetic" became for me a laboratory in which I could experiment with some concepts taught and demonstrated by Graham Cooke, Larry Randolph, Jim Goll, Michael Sullivant, James Ryle, and Randy Clark. I was hungering to know in my own experience what they were saying. As a result of their teaching and encouragement, I began to take ministry risks with a new confidence that God could and would speak through me as I remained a clean vessel for Him to use.

I also adopted certain protocols for ministering that I felt were biblical, safe, and sensitive to the needs of individuals. Henry Blackaby's advice pointed me inevitably in the direction I should go: "When you see the Father at work around you, that is your invitation to adjust your life to Him and join Him in that work." (*Experiencing God*, p. 64)

The results were powerful and immediate. During ministry time one evening at the conference, I was amazed—no, astounded!—at the precision with which the Holy Spirit spoke through me into the lives of persons coming forward for prayer. I didn't feel compelled to have some kind of revelation for these men and women, but I was absolutely filled with compassion for them. It was like my heart was beating in rhythm with the heartbeat of the Savior, and I was feeling His great love and mercy for His children. There was no need to say, "Thus saith the Lord," in an attempt to authenticate what I spoke. It was just as Larry Randolph had said: Old Testament prophetic activity was information received, while New Testament prophetic activity is information perceived. All I needed to do was gently say what I was sensing and let Father speak whatever it was that they needed to hear or know.

Most of the time this was just a comforting word about a particular personal situation, which reassured them that the Lord knew their situations and really cared for them. They were not flotsam and jetsam tossed out into a sea of adversity to bob on the waves of chance. No, the great "I Am" loved them, and He loved them so much that He would inspire me as I was praying for them to speak a word that confirmed how special they were to Him. As a result there was healing: emotional, physical, and spiritual.

The Lord worked out the trip details for Salem perfectly. Needing to be in the northeast on college business, I arranged my travels (with my vice-president's concurrence) so that Salem would fall right between meetings in Philadelphia and Boston. Not only that, but I would also be able to spend three evenings in Philadelphia with Randy Clark and Gary Shelton just prior to going to Salem. Randy was nearing the end of a thirty-day ministry in inner-city Philly at Deliverance Evangelistic Church. I would fulfill my college appointments during the day, then participate in services and ministry at night.

These three days functioned as a strategic, last-minute battle review. I had an opportunity to share my testimony at the meetings, as well as work in the deliverance room. Randy brought me forward, calling the congregation to an extended time of prayer and intercession for Salem. That evening, during personal ministry, a woman came to me for prayer. As I prayed for her, I felt a sharp pain in my lower abdomen between my navel and left-hip socket that caused me to grimace and stoop. As I did, the Holy Spirit told me, "This is not your pain. It's hers."

When I pointed to my abdomen and asked, "Are you experiencing pain in this area—a pain from colitis or diverticulitis?" she shrieked and staggered backwards. "Yes, yes, I suffer from diverticulitis!"

I said, "Father has revealed this to me, so that you will know that He will heal you. In the name of Jesus, I come against this infirmity and say to you, be healed."

She staggered again, then began to rock back and forth declaring, "I am healed, I am healed!" Tears streamed down her cheeks as she lifted her hands in praise. I continued, "It's important that you have this healing medically verified, then testify publicly to what

God has done. It doesn't matter who prayed for you. That's not important. What matters is that Jesus gets all the glory."

When I checked my e-mail two days later, I read an update from the Philadelphia meetings. It described a woman who testified that someone received a word knowledge about her diverticulitis and prayed for her healing. She gave great glory to God and brought with her a doctor's report verifying her healing. Praise the risen Lamb!

By the time I boarded the shuttle flight to Boston, I felt like the Lord had taken me through a spiritual battle simulator. But now I knew that we were well beyond simulation stage. This was the real thing: D-Day. The invasion was beginning. Many of God's people from around the world already had joined the battle, fasting and praying for what would occur in Salem. They were preparing the way for my arrival.

It was critically important for me to communicate with the prayer troops about how things were going. As we moved throughout the coming week's events, I felt that specifically targeted prayers would be vital weapons—spiritual smart bombs—in the arsenal against darkness. I would update as many prayer warriors as I could via e-mail and telephone. My e-mail updates became news from the front as well as the log that recorded victories as they came.

Friday 10/25/96

Dear Praying Friends,

I have just returned from walking the city of Salem, Massachusetts. For almost three and a half hours, Pastor Ken Steigler of Wesley United Methodist Church and I have circled the city and prayed. There are literally thousands of deceived children of darkness here. City-official vehicles, to include police, fire, and utility, have witches painted in the logo. Key posts in all departments of government are held by witches or warlocks. Great darkness is in this city. Between 600,000 and 800,000 people parade through here the last two weeks of October every year, and there is increased oppression.

But there already has been a breakthrough. Pastor told me how great heaviness lifted—the heavens were broken open five days ago. Believers here felt relief they had never known during this time of the year. Last weekend was the worst storm in over one hundred years with torrential rains and flooding. It completely washed out the three-day psychic fair! I stood at 160 Bridge Street and observed the ruins of the Parker Brothers game factory where Ouija Boards used to be made, until they went bankrupt about five years ago! As I watched further demolition of the site, I sensed God saying that the kingdom of darkness is coming down, that this is symbolic of a victory begun in the heavenlies a long time ago. There is an air of great expectancy that God is going to empower the Church to regain ground lost in 1972 when witch Laurie Cabot claimed Salem for Darkness.

Today I saw more evidence of Light. Walking down the street, I sensed with a genuine knowing that the advance party—heavenly warriors—were already here. At one corner I started to laugh because I knew in my spirit that a squad of angels was holding back the darkness at an acupuncture office. There was a recognition contact in the spiritual. Angels have been released in response to the prayers and intercedings of the saints, and they have infiltrated this area en masse. A great ground war is about to begin, and when the trumpet sounds, darkness will be routed.

Prayers originating from around the world have been like the carpet bombing conducted prior to the ground invasion of Operation Desert Storm. For days, B-52's from the air and battleships from the gulf delivered relentless fire upon southeastern Iraq where the Republican Guards were positioned. In military terms, this was considered "prepping the battlefield." It demoralized the enemy, brought confusion, and broke their will to win. Continue to lay down prayer fire. We must retain air superiority to win the battle.

Tonight I begin preaching at Wesley Church. There is a contemporary Christian music concert, and I will speak. PRAY, PRAY, PRAY for Jesus to conquer.

To war!
Harvey Brown

Sunday 10/27/96

I preach today at 10:00 a.m. and 6:00 p.m., and will be with an Hispanic congregation at 3:00 p.m. Worship will be led by Jim Spencer/Surrendered Heart.

No service was conducted last night. Instead, there was a time of personal ministry with the pastor and members traveling with the music ministry.

Pray especially for the pastor, the Reverend Ken Steigler, and his wife Marilyn. In the five and a half years he has been here, there has been consistent attack. Death threats are recurring (even the Bishop is called, and threats on Ken are made through him), bullets through the church windows, lawsuits (one currently has 41 counts against him), satanic graffiti, harassment. Yet in the midst of this, he is filled with Christ's love—and JOY.

Ken has the longest tenure of any Christian pastor in the city. Pastors here just don't last. Our Lord has upheld him and strengthened him, but he continually needs the prayers of saints worldwide.

GREAT NEWS. Your prayers are having profound effect. Ken reports that the presence of evil seems to be breaking over the city. Crowds are down significantly, and believers are encouraged as never before. More, Lord! Please continue to pray. We must relentlessly pursue victory for and through the power of the King.

Blessings,
Harvey Brown

Sunday Night 10/27/96

Dear Praying Friends,

THE HEAVENS ARE SHAKING! I am completely amazed (but not the least bit surprised) how God is at work here in Salem. This morning I preached to 100 persons at the 10 a.m. service. There was a sweet presence of the Lord, as much of the time was devoted to congregational sharing around the results of the weekend's church family activities (bake sale, country fair, etc.). I sensed great grace upon this time (not sure why, other than the fact that it reflected corporate life and a shared experience among the believers).

Following the sermon, I invited the organist to come down from the choir loft and let me pray for her. Pastor had told me that twelve years ago she was driving a car when someone on an overpass threw a brick through her windshield. As a result of the accident, she faced a continuing battle with migraine headaches and other neurological problems. I spoke to her about the Lord's compassion and shared the story of the woman with the twelve-year issue of blood touching Jesus' garment and being healed. I anointed her with oil and asked Jesus to heal her. She was baptized in the Holy Spirit after she received healing prayer. When I opened ministry time for others to come, two men came for deliverance from masturbation and pornography while others came for healing.

As I prayed for another woman, I sensed that she had been abused. When I asked her about it, she began to cry and acknowledged that she had been abused. As I spoke a healing word to her, I also sensed that she was not saved. I asked her if she knew Christ. She said no, asked Jesus into her life and was gloriously saved and baptized in the Holy Spirit. I called her son (approximately 11 years old) and led him to the Lord as well. The lady manifested unusual joy and praise. Pastor Ken shared with me on the way home that she had gotten into adultery and had an illegitimate child—and had placed a court injunction against the church to keep her son away from this "Christian cult." Today was the first time she had been in church for over two years. Jesus loved this wayward child into His eternal arms. What a sight, watching her sob in the pastor's arms after I had prayed for her and taken her to him, not knowing her past trauma! Jesus reigns!

I have just finished talking with the Hispanic pastor whose congregation meets here in the afternoon. I felt that the Holy Spirit wanted me to come minister to him. When we parted, he said that just this morning he told a sister that he was so discouraged that he needed a word from the Lord to be able to continue. I brought him that word. How wonderful that God would let this skinny gringo come from Kentucky to bless a needy servant of the King. Keep praying. Your prayers are having great effect.

In Him,
Harvey Brown

Monday Evening 10/28/96

Dear Praying Friends,

As I write this on Monday evening, I am grateful for the day of recovery from the weekend's battle. Today has been a day of refitting for tomorrow's fight. The battle has been severe, but great battles have meant great victories. I am especially lifted by the fact that some of you have taken the time to e-mail encouragement to me, letting me know of your prayers and intercessions. This has helped me to know how vast the call has been from the Lord for his Body to come together in warfare support for the assault on Salem and the powers of darkness. Please keep in touch. The battle continues to rage, and every word from you is like a resupply pipe line. More, Lord!

Tomorrow I will be in Boston for a luncheon with a brother, and tomorrow night I will begin three nights of ministry with worship musician John Polce. Please pray for us both.

Pastor Ken Steigler shared his perceptions of what has happened so far. Without exaggeration, he says that the breakthroughs for God's people here are the greatest he has seen in over five years of ministry in Salem. He says that believers, old and young, "…have been deeply moved, and are very thankful and touched by the honest and sincere love of Jesus Christ that they have sensed."

According to Ken, one young man—a new Christian who is a member of Wesley Church and an attendee of the Promise Keepers ministry—has great leadership potential. He is a former professional football player and YMCA Nautilus instructor. After Sunday worship, he told his pastor, "I never told anyone about what he prayed for—he just looked inside of me and spoke a cleansing word. I've never felt like this in my whole life!"

I learned more about Pam, the church organist of whom I wrote yesterday. Over the years she had undergone multiple tests to determine if anything could be done for the debilitating headaches she experienced as a result of the accident. She continued regular examinations and medication to no avail. Ken Steigler reported that after I prayed for her, she came to him with tears streaming down her cheeks. "My head is clear. I can think clearly! I can see clearly! My head doesn't hurt anymore!"

[Note: One year later, the report is the same—completely healed. Glory to the risen Lamb!]

And the forty-one-count indictment brought against Ken and his bishop by a disgruntled homosexual warlock has just been blocked!

Do prayers matter? Count on it. I do.

To war!

The blessings of the Savior be poured abundantly upon you.

Harvey Brown

Tuesday 10/29/96

Dear Brothers and Sisters,

Tonight was a close, intimate time of fellowship with Father and a small group of believers. John Polce shared tonight as our minister in music. He is a troubadour much like John Michael Talbot and Michael Card. What a blessing in Father's presence!

Tomorrow (today—Wednesday—when you read this) I will be going into the prison to preach at 2:00 p.m., then services start at the church at 7:00 p.m. Your prayers continue to open the breech in the dark oppression over this city. Light is breaking through as the Sun of Righteousness begins to shine. Thank you for all the cover.

Continuing in His battle,
Harvey Brown

Wednesday 10/30/96

Dear Praying Friends,

As I prepare for bed, my heart is singing with the angels over seven men who were saved today. I spoke in the prison near here to a multiracial group of inmates. After sharing Jesus' story of the prodigal son, I invited them to let Father run to them and restore them, to welcome them home and forgive them. For an invitation I challenged them not to bow their heads and close their eyes, but to look around at who would stand courageously for Christ. No secret believers can survive, only those who believe in their hearts AND confess with their mouths. Seven men stood, then prayed to receive Jesus.

I asked them if they would like to have people around the world pray for them. They gave me their names, along with some other brothers who wanted to be prayed for. Please list them before the Father.

Tonight's service was a precious time of worship and ministry from the Word. Tomorrow will be a major battle. Morning prayer from 9 a.m.-12 noon with area clergy, then tomorrow night with thirty churches and parachurch organizations to be on our faces before the Lord and receive the ministry of the Word. We are then taking it to the streets between 10 p.m. and 1 a.m. YWAM, students from Gordon-Conwell Theological Seminary, African American Churches from Boston, and local believers will pierce the darkness with the light of Christ. Please, KEEP PRAYING. I expect that the 6000+ witches, Satanists, santeria believers, and their demon hosts will oppose the work of God. Prayer and fasting are key weapons in this warfare.

I am much encouraged by your communications, prayers, and support. All glory goes to the Lamb, and remember: This is His victory through the cooperative efforts of His warring saints around the world.

IN HIS VICTORY!
Harvey Brown

Saturday 11/2/96

Salem Halloween Update

Dear Praying Friends,

I have never been more excited about what God is doing, nor more appreciative of the corporate nature of the Body of Christ. In the next few paragraphs I hope to be able to capture, however so partially, the enormity of the work of God in Salem, Massachusetts over the last few days.

Pastor Ken Steigler was ecstatic as he took me to the Boston airport at 4:30 a.m. Friday morning. All reports from those that went to the streets to share Christ were the same. Great receptivity to the gospel—almost as if people were waiting and wanting to hear about the love of

Christ. Salem had the quietest Halloween in decades. The atmosphere was more like a college fraternity party than a convergence of demonic forces. I believe—and those associated with the meetings for the last week concur—that the blanketing of prayer by saints around the world held back darkness. I AM MORE CONVINCED THAN EVER that the Church's failure to fast and pray over the years has been a major breech in her defenses against evil.

"Thank you" is an inadequate expression of my gratitude for your part in the assault on Salem. The victory is OURS through Jesus Christ. I hope you will share with everyone you know how Jesus was glorified in the darkness of Salem.

I spoke to the several hundred gathered during the Concert of Prayer at Wesley Church on Halloween. Theology students from Gordon-Conwell, YWAMers from New York—believers representing up to thirty different churches and parachurch organizations—were on their faces before the Lord. Several responded by coming to the altar to repent and confess secret sin. One theology student (among several who responded) sought deliverance from masturbation and pornography. Just that afternoon he had been looking at pornographic images on the Internet. He said that my message went straight to his heart and that he now had hope that God could and would set him free.

On the flight from Boston to Cincinnati, I had the privilege of leading my seat-mate to a saving knowledge of the Lord Jesus. Bob, an employee of John Hancock Insurance in Boston, was on his way to a meeting in Tampa. He's from a Catholic background, married to a Jewish woman named Laura, and has a two-year-old son named Benjamin. Please pray for the salvation of his entire family.

Attacks will continue against the saints, both within my own home and extended family as well as believers (especially Ken Steigler) in Salem. Please pray for my sixteen-year-old son, Harrison. He has had a difficult time while I was away, and my sense is that he is among the most vulnerable right now within my family.

I love you all, even though many of you I know only in the spirit. Be blessed by the Father. Salem is only one battle. The war continues. Praying for your own strength in the fight, I remain

Your faithful brother,
Harvey Brown

12

Final Exam at Asbury College

Never make a principle out of your experience; let God be as original with other people as He is with you. (Oswald Chambers)

The passing of time challenges our commitments—decisions made in a moment are tested in eternity. And it seemed like an eternity since I, while still a military chaplain, interviewed for a job with the president of Asbury College. The decisions I made that day were still shaping my future.

The president's question was a tough one…and very direct. If I accepted a position at Asbury College, would I be content in a role where I no longer preached regularly? I pondered my response for a moment before speaking. In the brief time that we had been together for my interview, I had already decided that I liked his leadership style. Dr. David Gyertson's perceptive, to the point, no-nonsense management style was tempered with a gentlemanly manner that made me look forward to joining his administration.

He has a real grasp of the issues, I thought. *I can work with him.*

With the exception of twenty-four months where I had military staff assignments, I had preached almost every Sunday for a quarter of a century. Becoming a college administrator would move me from the pulpit to the pew. "Honestly, sir, I don't know. But I do know this: I love Asbury College. It would be such an honor to serve here that I'm willing to put this aspect of ministry on the back burner for 3-5 years to commit to being part of your administration." I could not have imagined anything less. I anticipated a great deal more.

As days turned into weeks and months, I became acutely aware of the void left by not preaching regularly. I spoke only three times from June to December—once in chapel and twice at out-of-state commitments made before I left the Army. Being a college administrator was rewarding, but I was beginning to miss preaching. The longer I was away from the pulpit, the more I yearned to preach again.

I tried to mitigate my feelings by telling myself that the longer I was part of Asbury's staff, the more invitations I would eventually receive to preach. In the old days, many faculty and administration members would move throughout the country preaching in churches, revivals, and camp meetings. But that generation of preacher-academicians gradually had been replaced by uniquely academic types specializing in their intellectual disciplines. *The continuing demand among our constituents for preachers from the college would eventually catch up with me*, I reasoned. *Just cool your jets and wait.* However, this rationalization failed to satisfy the longing I felt for the pulpit.

This internal tug of war came to a head one cold blustery February day, as I fought a fierce wind while heading back to campus from the downtown barber shop. My wool scarf and hat were little use against the bone-chilling numbness that cut like a knife through my attempts at staying warm. As I reached campus, the chimes struck ten. Chapel was beginning. *God, thank You for letting me be here. Thank You for these young men and women who You are touching, even at this moment, and calling to serve You. Thank You, Father, for letting me be just a small part of that.* I started to weep. *And Father, if You want me here until I die—even if I never preach again—I will do whatever You want, wherever You want it. I relinquish to You my rights to the future. I'm in Your hands, Lord. Do with me what You will.*

At that moment, I knew it was settled. My struggle was now God's problem. But before the week was out I would understand in a new way what God had in mind to do with me.

* * * *

Ron's voice on the phone was so strained that at first I could hardly make out his words, but when he repeated himself, I understood: Ron Smith the evangelist was sick. "I've never canceled a meeting in my life," he whispered, barely audible, "but I'm just too sick to do anything. Is there any possible way that you can go to New Jersey and take some meetings for me?"

Wow. Four days ago I had surrendered my preaching to the Lord. Now He was handing it back. Maybe He wasn't through with my being a preacher after all.

Indeed, He wasn't. In less than eighteen hours I was on a flight to New Jersey, where I preached ten times in four days!

Over time, invitations to speak did become more regular, and after I experienced my renewal in the late spring, invitations really started increasing. As a result, I became concerned about any apparent conflict of interest between my role as an administrator at Asbury College and this emerging ministry that had potential to take needed time from my primary duties.

I talked candidly with both my vice-president and president about my concerns, and we negotiated clear guidelines about my extracurricular speaking engagements. We decided that I would use vacation days for all commitments that didn't directly relate to the college and that I would submit all invitations to the vice-president for approval. This accountability was important so that I could walk in integrity while attempting to blend two worlds: that of working in Christian higher education, and preaching.

The college supported me in different ways. They recognized the positive public relations value from having leaders preach in various venues. Not only did it advance recognition of the college and its programs, it also served as a drawing card for potential students. There were already several students attending Asbury because they had heard me speak. Something about what they heard had influenced them to enroll.

Also, as I began to speak more frequently in renewal circles and testify to God's miracles in my life, I became increasingly aware of the widening gap between constituencies of renewal and some constituencies of the college. I was certainly aware of the long-standing oral traditions of the college opposing charismatic phenomena, and there were even some college-related folk that actively spoke against such things. But I was also aware of many who welcomed and embraced the fresh winds of the Spirit blowing through renewal. It seemed to me that there certainly was room for renewal in holiness circles, and I readily saw that there was a need for holiness in renewal circles. I determined to attempt to walk a careful balance—trying to keep my feet in both.

I believed that an honest and open investigation of renewal would inevitably lead to the conclusion that God was actively involved. That is not to say that everything happening at a renewal meeting was of God, any more than everything happening at the First United Methodist Church was of God. But it is to say that to participate in wholesale denunciation of renewal as being ungodly and unnecessary is to demonstrate the intellectual integrity of flat-earth theorists. It is a denial of obviously recognizable fact.

Accordingly, I welcomed opportunities to discuss renewal and revival within the Church. In most places where I traveled, I found believers who hungered to know God in deeper and fuller ways. Although it was not my charter to shove renewal down folks' throats, neither was I going to avoid declaring the glorious and powerful work occurring in my life as a result of my power encounter with Him. I received from some people very warm and engaging responses. One of these came during the same trip where I met the Methodist district superintendent (who was a friend of renewal).

The trip's last leg took me to North Carolina. I had already arranged to share a hotel room with Dr. Robert Moore, chairman of the Department of Bible and Theology at Asbury College. Bob and I had known each other casually since playing intramural basketball together during graduate school. He was a gentle soul who had a keen mind and a pastor's heart.

We were reading in our hotel room when Bob said, "I understand that you've had some special experiences with the Lord recently." I was a little surprised to hear this, since my renewal experience had occurred just three weeks earlier. News certainly traveled fast. Not knowing what he thought about renewal, I was circumspect in my answer: "I sure have."

I couldn't determine much about what he thought by how he worded his question, and it seemed best not to volunteer too much. I decided to let him lead the conversation.

"My daughter told me about your sharing in church the Sunday after you returned from St. Louis. She said that it really touched her."

I then shared briefly with Bob what had happened to me and the changes that had taken place. However, I couldn't talk long because I needed to check out, so I handed him a copy of my e-mail testimony and said that we might talk later. In a few days I received a note from Bob, attached to my testimony. "I read your story with great interest," he wrote. "You and your family have experienced a profound and special blessing. I am happy for you and look forward to talking soon."

There were others in our community who felt decidedly different. Although I remembered the unsolicited comments and aspersions cast toward the Wilmore "Light the Fire" meetings, I didn't expect my association with renewal to evoke the same kind of antagonism. I mistakenly assumed that those strong feelings would diminish with time and understanding. My love for and service to the college would not be tarnished by my being deeply in love with the Savior and walking in His holiness. On the contrary, I had never been more fully equipped and ready to serve the King. The strong and vociferous opposition that arose from some alumni caught me completely off guard. In their minds, my identification with "Toronto" (even though I had yet to go there!) should put my job at risk.

* * * *

It was almost comical watching Peter[1] fidget in my office, telling me how dangerous it was to be involved in renewal. I had heard that he was an excellent speaker, and he preached regularly as an evangelist with a holiness evangelistic association in our town. But his thoughts seemed to be all over the map. He was clearly agitated and unsure of how to communicate his concerns. Slipping into counseling mode, I tried to help him clarify the issues.

As best I could determine, a friend of Peter's had sent him a copy of my "Dancing in the Fire" e-mail. I knew immediately to whom he was referring: I had met his friend Tom, a Methodist pastor, in Chattanooga. Tom had attended the services there, as well as the pastors' luncheon—never raising any questions, never asking for clarifications, never articulating any doubts or concerns. Yet two months later, out of concern for Asbury College, he sent my testimony to his friend in Willmore. And now Peter sat in my office, expressing some "grave misgivings."

"It's dangerous, Harvey," said Peter, "just dangerous. You need to be very careful about being involved with this kind of people."

I tried to reassure Peter that I was indeed in control of my faculties and that I loved the Lord more than ever. I told him that I could see his concern and appreciated his initiative in talking to me.

Peter had one more thing to add: "Well, I know I'm not going to be the only one. You'll probably be getting a call from Robert[2] too." I couldn't really tell if Peter's words were a warning, or a threat.

Robert served as the administrative head, as well as an evangelist, for the same organization to which Peter belongs. Although we

---

1. Name has been changed.
2. Name has been changed.

were not friends, I knew him on a professional level. Since I took seriously our Lord's admonition to be reconciled to a brother who might have anything against me, I called Robert, and he agreed to come by my office.

The air was palpably tense when he entered. I sat in a chair across from him as he handed me a letter. "I want you to read this first, if you would." Where Peter had been all over the map, Robert was right to the point: His letter was a forceful three-page document ending with the words, "I am greatly grieved that you are determined to be a trailblazer for this theology at Asbury. I only pray that I can do something to stop its onslaught before we lose our identity and ultimate contribution to the body of Christ and the world for which Asbury was raised." As an active and interested alumnus, he felt obligated to express his concerns to the president. Robert had also sent a copy to Dr. Gyertson.

I looked up at Robert. "It's a well-written document, and I can see clearly where you stand. But you need to know that it's full of hyperbole, exaggeration, and plain inaccuracies." At that point, I took the time to work through the letter and explain to Robert where he had quoted my paper out of context, drawn faulty conclusions, and accepted hearsay for fact. We then debated in a reasoned way the nature of renewal and the heritage that we shared.

At one point, I said, "I can tell that you are angry. But I also know that if you scratch an angry person deeply enough, you'll find someone who cares a great deal. I can tell that you care, Robert. You care about this school, you care about truth, you care about God's Church. But what you need to know is that I care every bit as passionately as you. We are really very close in many of these concerns."

I could see him starting to relax a little. "Come on, brother. Let's try to find where we agree and build from there."

For the next four hours, we discussed, debated, shared, and wept together. As our conversations drew to a close, I asked Robert to do one important thing for me. "You demonstrated real moral courage to come to the mat with me over these issues. Many people wouldn't have bothered, and now we understand each other in a new way. But since you have copied this letter to my president, would you also write a retraction of those points that you now know to be in error?" Robert agreed to the necessary retractions, and I received a copy of his new letter the next week.

Although that meeting went fairly well, I came away realizing that these issues were not about to go away. My antagonist was now more informed about the facts, but he remained convinced that I was too far from the mainstream to be a part of the administration. According to his words, we were now at an impasse.

I now knew firsthand the energy that existed around renewal issues among some constituents. And I discovered in discussions with folks who had moved into renewal from other traditions that many of them had experienced similar encounters. Religious passions can sometimes be very volatile. Occasionally they are completely irrational.

One evening I met with a former senior editor of *Christianity Today*. For two and a half hours, we discussed candidly his thoughts and feelings about renewal. I was surprised at how transparent this imminently respected Christian leader was—and how completely irrational he became when talking about Pentecostals and charismatics. At one point, he made a sweeping denunciation of charismatic character: "There is, Harvey, something that happens within a man when he has a charismatic experience that severs his ethical nerve." I grieved for my friend and mentor who had so offhandedly dismissed anyone who was of this persuasion.

During all of these events, I remained in close and constant communication with my president. Dr. Gyertson took the position that there was nothing in my theology or experience that should disqualify me from serving the college. In a letter, he stated, "Harvey's hunger to experience all of Christ led to a profound encounter with the cleansing, empowering work of the Spirit. While this encounter occurred outside his historic connection and experience, the fruit of this work is, in my opinion, consistent with our basic beliefs about

Entire Sanctification. Except for some of the ecstatic trappings, Harvey emerged from this encounter with a new freedom from the roots of sin, a passion for the Great Commission, and love for God and his fellow man characteristic of the best of our Holiness tradition."

In an effort to minimize the controversy's effects, we decided that I should maintain a low profile. I would focus on administrative tasks close at hand and cut back on my travels representing the college. Perhaps by letting some time and distance pass before I was back on the road, we could reduce the irritation factor among some of our group.

However, I was becoming increasingly aware that too much institutional energy was being drained from necessary tasks in order to respond to alumni concerns about me. I began to identify with the man born blind, whom Jesus healed in John 9. As a result of a power encounter with the Savior, he found himself in the middle of a broiling controversy not of his making. His only real response to his interrogators was his testimony. Some people related to him pulled back in fear of what others would think. But in the long run, the acceptance that mattered most to him was that of Jesus. It was so with me as well.

Toward the end of the year, another very vocal detractor entered the fray and enlarged the arena. A staff member from a mega-church in a southern state wrote a scathing letter to the president about my testimony and sent copies of his letter—as well as my testimony—to the entire Board of Trustees. I couldn't help but think, *Here we go again.* I was becoming weary of this continuing and apparently endless controversy.

In some ways I was struggling to make sense out of everything going on. I knew that God was on the throne and that He had a plan for my life. I had no doubts about the fact that the Lord led me to Asbury College and called me to this administration. Yet, on the other hand, I knew that I was being extruded into a ministry of renewal that was more powerful than anything I had ever experienced before. I was seeing dramatic results every time I spoke, especially when I shared my testimony of freedom from the strong-holds of sexual bondage. My heart was increasingly drawn toward proclamation of the Good News. Plus there were some very specific things that the Lord had spoken prophetically into my life concerning the dimensions of future ministry.

I was facing a real dilemma over staying at the college. If I left the college to pursue a new ministry of renewal, I ran the risk of leaving prematurely and possibly missing God's will for me as part of the administration. On the other hand, if the Lord were calling me to leave, my needs for security and predictability might cause me to miss His will for me to speak. In my heart, I knew that changes would come eventually, but I had no clue as to proper timing.

Only one thing was certain: I wanted nothing but Father's perfect will.

In some ways, this tension was immobilizing. I really wasn't free to immerse myself completely in renewal, because I respected my president and the leadership predicament he was in. Until there was some final resolution in my status, I needed to remain sensitive to the implications of my actions. I chose to decline an invitation to share my testimony during a healing conference in Toronto, figuring that there would be time for this later.

Neither was I free to throw myself wholeheartedly into the college's work. With all of the negative energy directed toward me in some circles, my effectiveness with key segments of our alumni was completely emasculated. It seemed that I spent much time at my desk, just staring into space trying to grasp what the future held. The first Monday in March finally brought the answer.

I knew that something was up when the president's secretary called to make an appointment for me with Dr. Gyertson. Because my office was directly across the hall, we would generally just walk into each other's office. But this was formal.

Dr. Gyertson invited me to sit at the small conference table, then handed me a two-page memorandum, beginning with "Subject:

Discontinuation of Employment." My heart skipped a beat as I skimmed the letter. My job position had been eliminated. This was finally it—the answer to my questions about the future. God was moving me out. I felt a profound sense of relief.

The explanation was clear and reasonable, and had been brought up previously, so nothing was a surprise. My division had been undergoing a complete restructuring as we moved to a new model of institutional advancement, and the president had decided that my role was no longer needed.

But beyond that, David Gyertson had been on his face before the Lord. He sensed what God was doing and that, in order for me to be free to follow the Spirit's leadership, I had to be released from the college. He understood my passion for the gospel. The memo's closing sentence clearly revealed his feelings: "We are in prayer that God's next step will be into the depths of your heart's desire for effective ministry and service on behalf of His worldwide renewal."

To which I could add my own hearty "Amen."

13

Ministry With Maximum Impact

I am the vine; you are the branches. If a man remains in Me and I in him, he will bear much fruit; apart from Me you can do nothing. (Jesus)

I faced the prospect of an uncertain future with mixed emotions. I was relieved because now I knew how long I would remain at Asbury, but I also felt a subtle and somewhat insidious emptiness in my gut. For the last twenty-five years, I had carefully sculpted my identity from the institutional clay surrounding me. Harvey Brown was defined by where he worked: pastor, chaplain, college administrator. For the first time in my adult life, I lacked that definition. I felt like an embolism—a free-floating blood clot—in the Body of Christ. By no longer being at the college, I was adrift and unconnected. Not until another week had passed—when the announcement was made public—would I be free to discuss leaving Asbury with anyone but my family.

I looked forward to our small-group gathering on Wednesday. In the few weeks that we had been meeting, these dozen or so brothers and sisters from church had strongly bonded. Because of my group dynamics training, I could tell that we were making faster-than-average progress toward true group cohesiveness and deep trust. That night, one member brought multiple strands of small-gauge wire and told us to create a personal sculpture that said something about ourselves.

Been there, done that, I thought. *It's a classic group-type ice-breaker. Should be fun.*

I grabbed a few pieces of wire and started twisting, not really sure what I'd come up with but not really feeling any pressure either. Before I knew it, I had fashioned a question mark out of the wire. I smiled. That would keep them guessing, until it was my turn to share.

We made our way around the room, explaining our sculptures. When it came to my turn, I held up my question mark and said glibly, "I have some questions," then paused and said, "because I lost my job today."

I didn't mean to say that, I thought, surprised. The next thing that came out was a sob so loud that it startled even me. I suddenly began to cry and found myself gasping the words, "I need all of you so much."

Before I knew it, I was surrounded by one huge hug. My brothers and sisters were holding me up—a visible symbol of what the Body was all about. When I could finally talk, I shared my whole story with them. Only in the presence of my friends did the full impact of what was happening hit me, but the strength I drew from them offered enormous comfort.

I had no doubts about what God's power had done in my life. The vision had been real, and I was seeing its fulfillment almost immediately. The Lord had also spoken plainly about an emerging worldwide ministry to which He was calling me, and I had been seeing demonstrations of the Holy Spirit's power with dramatic regularity. It wasn't that I didn't trust God. It was that I didn't trust me. Just like Moses, who came up with every excuse in the Book as to why he was unsuitable for God's purposes, I suddenly found myself overwhelmed by my own sense of inadequacy and wanting to negotiate terms of surrender with God. I knew that if I would ever make any Kingdom impact, I would need Aarons (God, give me Aarons!) to walk with me. But even before I was aware of my need, God had been meeting it. My friends' arms were my Aarons. I wasn't just floating...I was truly connected to my local Body of Christ.

Released from college, I was now free to enter wholeheartedly into renewal ministry. Trusted friends and advisers had urged me the previous year to incorporate a ministry organization, so that I could have a clean break between my college and separate ministry work. When it came time to select a ministry name, I sat there with the Articles of Incorporation in my hand and breathed a prayer. "What would You have me name this, Father?"

I didn't hear any response, so I prayed again. "What would You have me name this, Father?"

In my spirit, I heard the Lord speak. "You won't name this anything."

That didn't make sense.

"You won't name this anything," repeated God, "because I have already called this ministry by name."

Then a bright light shone through my darkened memory, and I recalled the final words of prophecy spoken over me by Jim Goll in St. Louis: "I just speak impact ministries. I don't know what it is, but it will come about sometime. I just say 'Impact ministries' to you."

I contacted my researcher at the college and asked her to run a national trademark search on the name "Impact Ministries." The next day I received the results: No one else had used the name—at least until now. God had called me, and this ministry, by name.

Now I realized I was sitting there with a ministry name, a vision of renewal, a calendar with no engagements written on it—and the most extraordinary peace that I had ever felt. I sensed that the Lord was about to unfold my future just as someone would unfold a roadmap and lay it out to examine. Any door could now become an open door; I just needed to learn how to walk through.

It seemed wise to contact others involved in full-time traveling ministries, to research the problems, pitfalls, and possibilities of life on the road. I had no need or desire to reinvent the wheel: Many other folk did this all the time, so why not glean from their knowledge and experiences?

I thought of Barry Perez, a good friend of twenty-five years. Barry had headed the International Christian Embassy and also served as an associate evangelist with Bazil Howard-Browne. When he invited me to be his guest at some Ohio meetings, it seemed like a wonderful opportunity to understudy a successful evangelist and to model Impact Ministries after a proven pattern. I was curious as to how he opened a series of meetings, developed momentum, and managed mechanical and logistical considerations. Having accepted his invitation, I was preparing to clean up and hit the road in time to attend the first service.

While showering, I was partly thinking and partly praying when I realized I had not even asked God about my going. Here I was, about to launch a faith ministry that had to be completely dependent on Father's hand, guidance, and provision, and already I had stepped to the helm and started to steer!

Oh Lord! I thought. *I'm so sorry. I've been charging ahead and forgot to look where You were going. I really want Your guidance...nothing but exactly what You want me to do. I can't be in control—Lord I won't be in control. You lead, Lord, for Your glory alone, You lead... I will follow.*

The Lord, the God of the universe, then clearly spoke to me: "I do not want you to go. You are looking to men to shape your ministry, and you can. But I want to shape My ministry in you. You are not to pattern yourself after any man. Follow Me." On my knees in the shower, with fresh water cascading across my shoulders, I was also being washed by my Father—cleansed from the residue of self-directed living.

During my devotions the following Thursday, the Lord spoke to me again and told me to join Barry for the last two days of meetings. I got to Ohio just in time for the evening service. I heard a different man than I had known in the past. I had loved Barry for a long time but had never seen the anointing of God on him like that night. He invited me to pray alongside him during ministry time, and together we began to move among the crowd responding to the invitation.

At one point, Barry asked if I were hearing anything from the Lord. I sensed that the Lord was revealing something about a ministry couple—that everything looked alright on the outside but was falling apart on the inside because of a fractured relationship. God wanted to heal their marriage. When Barry handed me the microphone to share this word, I felt the power of the Holy Spirit amplify what I was sharing. During the rest of the evening as I ministered, there was a continual flow of revelatory gifts that powerfully touched some deeply scarred areas of people's lives.

The following night was the last service of the week. Worship had finished and it was time for Barry to step onto the platform when he turned and said, "Harvey, I believe the Lord wants you to preach tonight. Will you do it?"

I looked at Barry and laughed. "Sure, brother."

I clipped the lavaliere microphone to my shirt while Barry gave me a brief introduction. In moments, I was standing in front of several hundred people and feeling very vulnerable. I'm not really a control freak, but I am much more comfortable when I'm prepared and ready. What I hadn't learned yet was that, although I had been caught offguard by the situation, Father wasn't the least bit surprised. I opened my mouth and began to share Revelation 12:11: "They overcame him by the blood of the Lamb and by the word of their testimony; they did not love their lives so much as to shrink from death."

For the next sixty minutes I shared the testimony of my renewal and deliverance from sexual bondage. During that hour I died again. I died to pride. I died to reputation. I died to self. Telling my story publicly was like driving more nails into the coffin of the old man. When I finished, I invited men who wanted to be free to come to the altar. From all over the church, suddenly men began to run toward the platform. There was no age qualifier: Young and old alike responded. I saw the sound engineer throw his headphones onto the tape deck and jump out of the sound booth. He ran down the aisle and dove onto the floor at the front of the church as a spirit of repentance moved in waves across the congregation. An act of surrender—mine—caused victory after victory to be won.

Father was so merciful: Through my dying, others were called to life.

On the way home, I was driving south on I-77 when I passed a huge billboard suspended a hundred feet above the concrete, its gaudy gold letters on black background screaming "ADULT BOOKS AND VIDEOS." Underneath it were the smaller words, "Right behind the Liberty Truck Stop."

As I passed the sign, I began to weep and plead to the Father on behalf of those men and women who were there. I knew what they were experiencing. I knew what it felt like to be driving down a road and be confronted with a pornographic message and to feel your heart beat faster and to sense the presence of a claw in your gut. I knew what it was like to be attracted to the very thing that repulsed you. I knew what it was like to be a slave to sin.

And now I knew what it was like to be gloriously free.

How ironic, I thought. *Right behind the Liberty Truck Stop. It's not liberty. It's bondage, bondage, bondage.*

Words from a Charles Wesley hymn flooded my mind:

Long my imprisoned spirit lay fast bound in sin and nature's night.
Thine eye diffused a quickening ray, I woke, the dungeon flamed
with light.

My chains fell off, my heart was free. I rose, went forth and followed thee.[1]

I really was free. And it became increasingly clear to me that one of the things Father was going to do through my ministry would be to break chains through the impact of my testimony.

I would discover in days ahead that the vicious grip of sexual bondage was pervasive—that the number and frequency of persons struggling with different kinds of sexual addictions is staggering. As I connected with other ministries, I uncovered startling statistics. Stan Kellner, from Focus on the Family's Pastoral Ministry Division, told me that over half of the calls they receive from clergy each day deal with sexual misconduct and marital concerns. And the more I listened to other informed voices, the more I realized that this problem permeates the Church—because it permeates the world, and the world has permeated the Church. One major ministry recently began to monitor employee Internet usage and discovered five employees (including two executives) accessing Internet pornography through their work computers.

This is also a problem we've laid on our children. John and Carol Arnott invited me to Toronto over Easter 1997 to share my testimony during the spring break youth conference. After a 14-hour trip, we arrived in Toronto, shortly before I was scheduled to share during the main session. When I stepped onto the platform, I felt very tired and very old: a balding middle-aged academic about to tell my story to kids who wore pierced earrings in places that I wouldn't even expose. I looked out at three-thousand-plus young people from around the world who were waiting to hear what I had to say. It is so difficult to describe the power of the Holy Spirit that was present. All I can say is that prayers were answered as God did many miracles in the lives of His children.

The following comes from Nicky Cantelon, wife of Todd Cantelon—one of the youth speakers at the conference:

---

1. "And Can It Be That I Should Gain?" by Charles Wesley (Public Domain).

"I was amazed at what I saw last night at the Toronto Airport Christian Fellowship. Following Harvey Brown's testimony, I watched hundreds of young people respond to a call for a release from lustful chains. As I stood at the front, I watched a *constant* flow of young men and women come forward to repent from masturbation, pornography, and the double life that sin causes. As a young person myself, I see the destruction that this particular sin produces in the lives of loved ones around me. I thank the Lord that God has chosen to raise up people like Harvey to die to themselves and let God's children know that they don't need to live double lives any longer. I believe that the Lord is going to continue to work through Harvey. And I'm praying for my generation to repent from their ways—for many others to be raised up to give their testimonies as Harvey has done so powerfully and effectively."

The Lord also moved upon a group of clergy leaders when I keynoted a leadership retreat in Lancaster, Pennsylvania, later that month. I was given time after supper on Tuesday to address what God was doing in the world today. I identified what I labeled as five streams of renewal that—if viewed together—resemble a river that might be a revival. My lecture's thesis was that, if history were to afford us the opportunity to reflect on these days, we might discover that this was the beginning of the Last Great Awakening. I talked about the men's movement, prayer and fasting movement, Toronto, the move of God in the 10/40 window, and Pensacola. I also alluded to my own renewal.

We were scheduled to adjourn following thirty minutes of worship at 8:30, but the participants were so energized by what I shared that they asked to reconvene. During the unscheduled second session, I played a portion of a videotape of my testimony in Toronto. The Lord used it to break open the hurting hearts of these pastors, and we went directly into a personal prayer ministry that lasted until after midnight.

At lunch the next day, a pastor from Delaware told me that he felt like the Lord Jesus tailored the meeting exclusively for him.

"On my way here, I prayed over and over that God would set me free from double-mindedness. Everything that I needed was what you shared. You came here just for me."

A Pennsylvania pastor wrote "Praise be to God! These past two days have been a time of spiritual cleansing and renewal: a refining process to wash by the blood of Jesus impurities from my soul…. A time of refreshing my spirit and putting excitement back in…for getting God's direction to use me as He wills. Come, Holy Spirit, and refresh Your people as You have refreshed me!"

Five days later, I again saw evidence of our Father's love for His children when I preached in a Methodist church in Virginia. Judy Knight, wife of pastor David Knight, captured some of what she sensed God doing.

"Services have been very much anointed by the Holy Spirit…God is healing and setting free those in bondage. Monday night, a word of knowledge was given by Harvey that someone was suffering from a specific condition. My friend was sitting next to me. She began to shake and said, 'Judy, that's me!' She ran to the front and received a powerful touch from the Lord. She is having tests on Monday, and we believe that the doctors will find nothing wrong and that she is healed. [Update: Doctors found nothing wrong with her.] What an encouragement to my friend that God knows her, loves her, and wants to heal her…There is so much balance in Harvey's ministry. What a blessing!"

When I came away from the Virginia meetings, I had another huge blessing. In my billfold was a four-figure check—the honorarium for the meetings. When I had first opened the envelope and looked at the check, my immediate response was "YES! Thank You, God! This is for June!" I knew that I was facing a precipitous drop in income as I left the college and stepped out in faith, and this was surely God's provision for the first month.

Four days later I was worshipping in my local church. It felt great to be back with my brothers and sisters after several weeks of traveling. Just prior to taking the offering, our pastor reminded us that for the last month the leadership had been seeking God about our budget and wondering whether we should stretch a little more (we were already giving thirty percent to missions right off the top) or whether we should pull back. He spoke of how the morning's offering would signal what we should do.

As the ushers made their way to the front, I thought to myself, *If I had remembered, I would have cut a special check for today. Sure wish I had something to give.* As soon as those words formed in my mind, the Lord spoke to my heart: "You do."

I knew what He meant. I was about to take a crash course in God's school of economics.

Folded carefully in my billfold was the honorarium check. Next month's groceries and mortgage payment. The kids' high-school graduation presents. My heart was pounding in my chest, and I started to cry. God was speaking to me.

"Am I your source, or is it that check? Do I not own everything? I will provide for you, but not for you alone. I will provide enough for you to give to others as I tell you to. Hold all things loosely."

I could feel something starting to break from me. A spirit of poverty was being ripped away. Four days before, I didn't have this money; God did. If He chose to use me to pass it to someone else, then why not? As a steward, I just manage something that's not my own anyway. All money belongs to God. I didn't need to grasp for provision, because I was a friend of Jehovah-Jireh.

I endorsed the check and dropped it into the plate, then fell to my face on the floor and sobbed. So what if I was the only person in church on the floor during the offering? So what if my sobs competed with the offertory being played on the electric piano? I was dying again so that I could be raised a new man—a man who was free indeed.

This new freedom has been more than a paradigm shift—I'm describing the process as moving the grid to an entirely different map sheet because Jesus just keeps rocking my world. Sometimes He even tells me in advance what's coming.

For example, in a prophecy spoken over me in October, Randy Clark said that he saw me speaking at a Methodist seminary in Europe. Six months later I received an unexpected invitation to preach for a week at the Baltic Methodist Theological Seminary in Tallinn, Estonia (a Baltic state formerly part of the Soviet Union), as well as speak at a national Christian gathering that will be simultaneously translated into Russian, Finnish, and Estonian. Father has given me a heart for missions and emerging churches, so now Impact Ministries has sent its first missionary intern to Central America.

And I have had a blinding flash of the obvious. When Jesus was talking to Peter about the Church, He said that the gates of hell would not prevail against it. A gate is part of a defensive fortification. For too long, the Church has barred *its* gates and tried to keep out the world, the flesh, and the devil. But we are supposed to be on the offense—moving out of our fortresses and gaining ground by taking captive every evil imagination. A major evangelistic push is being prepared to recapture more territory by taking worship to the streets in a city dedicated to darkness.

There is so much more that I could share but little time or space to capture all that I have seen the Lord do. Yet one thing is clear to me in these examples I have shared: God is leading me into a broader and more profound ministry than I could have ever imagined.

The design of the Impact Ministries logo includes a heart that's on fire. I can't imagine it being any other way because my own heart has been strangely warmed. God struck a match that set it on fire with a passion for holiness and renewal.

Epilogue

Sir, Do I Perceive
a Speck in Your Eye?

The fact of the matter is that, while Christians may enter into this fuller life by different ways, provided Christ is their center, we need not regard their experiences or doctrines as mutually exclusive, but rather complementary. (Watchman Nee)

Every move of God has detractors. Some are malicious men with evil hearts, while others are godly men who are misguided or misinformed. Beloved and mature Christian leaders can, when left to their own judgment, mistake the works of God for flesh—or even worse, for the devil. In his book *From Holy Laughter to Holy Fire*, Dr. Michael Brown points out that G. Campbell Morgan—one of the most respected Bible teachers of the early twentieth century—described the 1906 Azusa Street outpouring as "the last vomit of Satan." Another highly regarded Christian leader, H.A. Ironside, scored both the modern Holiness and Pentecostal movements as "disgusting...delusions and insanities."

The presence of detractors of renewal in my story in no way negates the long standing Kingdom contributions that Asbury College has made in the past—or the contributions it will make in the future. What their presence plainly illustrates is how difficult it can be for individuals and institutions to respond to current moves of

God. There is an inherent inertia in every organization, no matter how spiritual, that keeps the institution moving forward in its prescribed direction. It's like trying to push a car to get it started. In the beginning, a great deal of effort is needed to get the thing moving, but once it gets rolling, it develops its own momentum. I believe that detractors are genuinely concerned that injecting new movements into institutional life might derail the organization (be it local church, parachurch, college or seminary) from its initial purpose. For some Asbury alumni, my presence symbolized the potential to get the college off-track.

But for others, my presence served an altogether different purpose. The President and Trustees, even before I had come on staff, had begun a process of questioning whether Asbury needed to broaden its position and link hands with other traditions while maintaining its distinctives. For these people, my presence was a catalyst that precipitated further review of why we existed and how we came to be. It was like God was using my situation as a lens to help people focus on what He was doing in the world, and then consider if He had anything to say regarding to how we conducted His business. Asbury's administration and its Board of Trustees were compelled to take an even closer look at the college. We needed to examine our institutional beliefs, customs, and policies by holding them up to the Light to see if we were walking in harmony with the Spirit of God.

Throughout history, people at the cutting edge of whatever God is doing may well be labeled "extremists." According to Jim Goll, territory is never taken by people of balance: it's always taken by extremists. People of balance maintain the territory once it is taken. The Body of Christ needs both extremists to pioneer God's new works and people of balance to maintain and perpetuate the institutions that result from victories won. But we must remember that pioneers are, by definition, "imbalanced."

The reality is that Holiness movement pioneers were shouting, marching, falling-down believers who hungered for God enough to travel great lengths to attend primitive camp meetings and seek the presence of the Holy Spirit. These believers labored at the altar to pray through, get the blessing, and know the power. They went around the world with missionary zeal and bore the reproach of cynical and disbelieving people. They founded schools to honor the Bible, pursue the doctrine and experience of holiness, and train young hearts in the ways of truth. They rejected the faithless liberalism of their age and swam against the tide of modernism. The institutions that these pioneers founded are now run, maintained, and supported by people of balance who work diligently to maintain that balance—and the associated respectability. Yet care must be taken that we in our balance never forget that we were born through a radical Spirit-led zeal.

Institutions also nurture and perpetuate old doctrinal and theological conflicts long after the battles are fought and the outcome determined. At the turn of the century, the Holiness movement held the franchise on the Person and work of the Holy Spirit. As various individuals and groups within the movement sought to go deeper with God, they experienced a fresh outpouring—and glossolalia. But the Holiness movement chose to separate itself from tongues speakers and took great pains to distance itself from these segments of the Body of Christ.

The more I moved throughout Holiness circles, the more I discovered the vestiges of this nearly century-old conflict. Even though many Asburians were in harmony with charismatic and renewal type experiences, there was a significant and very vocal constituency that was still fighting old battles, not embracing the massive contributions of Pentecostal and charismatic Christians to the world-wide cause of Christ. We even had alumni who wanted to forbid anyone who had spoken in tongues from attending or teaching at the college. What they fail to comprehend is their position would disqualify Paul from teaching theology—or Matthew from working in fund-raising. They don't consider the fact that God has chosen to work powerfully around the world through other traditions as well as their own.

Historical theologians would probably agree that in terms of movement, the Holiness movement (as well as others) has run its course and God is now renewing His Church in a different way. If they were to get close to the current movement, they would discover that large segments of today's renewal are honoring traditions that the Holiness movement has faithfully protected, nurtured, and preserved. Holiness leaders could be building bridges into emerging movements in the Church and speaking a much needed word—a sanctifying word of holiness of heart and life. As a new movement, we desperately need to discover this facet of the Father's heart for His Son's bride.

I don't want to sound like someone wildly dogmatic shouting back at people standing where he used to be. I too have seen the excesses and aberrations of renewal. But persons related to religious institutions like Asbury College—be they Methodist, Presbyterian, Disciples of Christ, or Pentecostal—need to remember that the institutions to which they have become accustomed were also born out of movements. Upon doing this, they may become more sympathetic toward newly refreshed souls who—even at the risk of violating institutional norms—fall drunkenly in love with the Savior.

One theme of the current renewal has been the breaking down of dividing walls. I know that this is Father's doing. He is revealing the mystery of His will according to His good pleasure...to bring all things in heaven and earth together under one head, even Christ (Eph. 1:9-10). A bottom-line theology is at work here: No matter how far we have come in the Kingdom journey, there is still further to go. As long as we remain outside of unity, we haven't gotten there yet.

God is in the business of making us whole. Just as biological children can mirror the genetic flaws of their parents—be it a large nose or tendency toward obesity—children of movements and institutions mirror those flaws as well. In some cases, seeing those flaws in others might be an indication that we may have them ourselves.

Recognizing and dealing with those flaws is a crucial step of the healing process.

There's nothing like a good crisis to force us to think. My presence at the college stimulated significant discussion and reflection, both within and beyond the campus, about who we were, where we came from, and where we were going. At a recent meeting of the Board of Trustees, one evening was dedicated to an open forum where the business agenda was set aside and Board members had an opportunity to share together and reflect on the college heritage. Two questions were posed to the Board: What are the distinctives—the positive things that make up the Asbury experience—and what are the negatives—the things about Asbury that cause bother or concern? About three-fourths of the Board took turns sharing from their own experiences around the first question. Touching and tender things were revealed as people told story after story about how the Savior had blessed them through this school.

When conversation shifted to issues that concerned Board members, one shared a fear that if the college let charismatic influences in, we might lose our distinctives. Another spoke up and said that it sometimes seemed that we were always fighting another group. Then a retired minister, an elder-statesman type, raised his hand and was recognized by the chairman. This is what he said:[1]

> "I hate to speak because I may open a can of worms, but I can't sit here and remain silent any longer. I was a young businessman who was doing quite well when I met Jesus and my life was changed. He called me to preach, so I picked up my wife and three children and began an Abraham's journey that brought me to Wilmore and Asbury College. I was like a sponge soaking up everything that I could about this new life in Christ. I established heroes—professors and mentors who guided and shaped me. I took everything from this place that I could...but it also included a fear of anything ecstatic. You might call

---

1. This account is based upon an extensive personal interview with the speaker. It is shared with his permission.

it 'charisphobia.' I almost preached it. I gave no charismatic person a chance.

"When I started my last pastorate I came to a church with a whole covey of charismatics. Many were self-righteous, and when I was around them I felt fear and paranoia. Before I was through with them, over a hundred had left the church. Some left because of unrest. Others left because they felt that the pastor hindered their Christian experience. I thought we could get along better without them. The church still grew and we became the largest-attended Methodist church in the state. But for years after this, I fought a battle deep inside of me: These people really loved the Lord, and I hadn't given them a chance, so they just slipped away.

"In 1991, my son was going to Anaheim, California, to attend a Vineyard conference. He invited me to go. I knew I needed some kind of healing and here was a chance to see the charismatic movement at its 'purest.' I had also heard that there was great worship. While I was there, I saw the charismatic movement in an entirely different fashion. I saw manifestations, but none offended me. Then the great holiness preacher Leonard Ravenhill spoke. Here were six thousand people hungry for more of Jesus and I had to ask myself, 'Do I see this now in the Holiness movement? Do I see this in my beloved Methodist church?' I found myself weeping...then sobbing. I didn't know what was happening to me, but after it was all over, I found myself healed."

Several Board members around the table were weeping gently at this point. The man continued to share, his own eyes brimmed with tears. "I now realize that I could have ministered to those people differently, had I not taken an unhealthy fear from this institution. We just didn't deal with it very well." He paused and looked around the room. "Do you remember how it all began for you? I wonder if there might be something ecstatic in our own experiences— something that was our own response to encountering God. I'm not talking about theology right now. All I'm asking is that we might be tolerant...and loving."

When reading this man's story, you might have said, "Right on, my church (school, institution, you fill in the blank) needs to be more tolerant and loving." Probably so.

But I pray that in renewal, as we reflect on our involvement with Christian institutions, we don't get so busy trying to remove the perceived speck in our brother's eye that we miss a plank in our own. I have talked with a number of people who have entered into renewal and felt rejection from "unrenewed" structures and persons around them. And in the pain of being rejected by their old world, they end up adopting a "Come out from among them and be ye separate" attitude—in essence, assuming a posture every bit as unloving and intolerant as the institution that they have just left.

While writing this book, I have had to be relentless in evaluating my own motives. If I were completely honest, I would admit that during some of my experiences I was tempted to pronounce "Ichabod" over my detractors and gather a sick little support group of misunderstood people to agree with me. But instead, I cried out to God and begged the Holy Spirit to show me His heart for those who at the time didn't see eye-to-eye with me. Jesus' prayer in John 17 is that we may be one, even as He and the Father are one. I yearn for the time when all of us who name the name of Christ can trust God enough to work in us what He wills, and not feel the need to recreate other believers in our own image.

Watchman Nee wrote:

If you ask a number of believers who have entered upon the fullness of life in Christ how they came by their experience, some will say in this way and some will say in that. Each stresses his own particular mode of entering in and produces Scriptures to support his experience; and unhappily many Christians are using their special experiences and special Scriptures to fight other Christians. The fact of the matter is that, while Christians may enter into this fuller life by different ways, provided Christ is their center, we need not regard their experiences or doctrines as mutually exclusive, but rather complementary. For one thing is certain: any experience of value in the sight of God must have been reached by way of a new discovery of the meaning of the person and work of the Lord Jesus. There is no other way. This is a safe test and a crucial one.[2]

May the mercies of God continue to test us—and purify us—as we long for His appearing. More, Lord!

---

2. Reading for November 21st. "A Table in the Wilderness: Daily Meditations From the Ministry of Watchman Nee," Watchman Nee, Christian Literature Crusade, Fort Washington, Pennsylvania, 1965.

If You Need Help

One of the central themes I continually hear (as I move among various parts of the Body of Christ) is a call for holiness of heart and life within believers. Father is calling his children to bring all areas of their lives under the authority of Christ. He is looking for a people who will serve Him with their hearts as well as their lips.

Part of my own story has been the recurring struggle with sexual issues—specifically masturbation and pornography—and a miraculous intervention by God that brought me a freedom I had sought unsuccessfully for years. I know what it's like to be trapped by the tandem twins of guilt and shame. I have agonized over my inability to live and walk victoriously in these areas. I fought a lonely and losing battle over these issues, longing for someone with whom I could risk myself yet wondering if anyone could really empathize and identify with my struggle—let alone genuinely help.

I want you to know that you do not have to deal with similar issues alone. By bringing your darkness to the light and seeking help, God can (and I truly believe He will) provide a way of escape. There are many resources, including Christian counselors and helping agencies, who can walk with you and help guide you into freedom and recovery. Your pastor can be a first stopping point in seeking help.

But if you are a Christian professional, as I am, you might find it exceedingly difficult to find someone with whom you are willing to risk yourself. The pastoral ministries division of Focus on the Family in Colorado Springs may have recommended resources in an area near you. Or perhaps, because of having read this book, you sense that I am someone with whom you can connect.

If that is the case, I want you to know that I am available to speak with you and assist, in whatever way I can, in helping you discover Christ's freedom. I know that this freedom is available—not only have I found it in my own life, but I have heard from others the testimonies of God's great mercy. Let me share one with you.

Dear Harvey,

Thank you and God bless you! My prayer is that God will abundantly bless you as you continue to die so that others might live. I pray that through this letter you will know some of the joy and freedom that I have experienced over the past 18 hours. I have never been ministered to with such compassion, gentleness, and acceptance. I felt so safe. The usual fear was gone. The Lord showed you every part of my struggle; the condemnation, the defeat, the fear, the embarrassment, the dread and hopelessness of ever being freed from the torment of my sin. Through you, the Lord Jesus reached down and set me free. Freedom to go on. Freedom to live again. Freedom to minister without condemnation. I have walked with this for years believing there was no one in the world who could help me carry the load. I knew that Christ had forgiven me because I had confessed my sin at least a million times. Now there is more—here is what Christ has done for me:

- given me an unspeakable and indescribable peace—the torment is gone.

- given me a joy that I have never experienced—the load is lighter—a song in my heart.

- given me the ability to surrender everything to Him—I lived in condemnation and was continually distracted by my sin—I lived in fear that He would require more of me than I could give (regarding confession). I now have the assurance that if He requires something more of me, He will give me the needed strength and courage.

- given me freedom to worship and minister without Satan blackmailing me with my sin. During worship, I always saw my sin and feared that others would find out what I really was.

- given me freedom to give myself wholly to my spouse—the secret and lie was a barrier I couldn't be freed from. Yesterday, Jesus gave me the opportunity to recommit myself and my sexual purity to my husband.

- given me the ability to trust someone with my life and believe in that trust—I believed if I shared this with someone I would live to regret it forever. Now I know trust.

- set me free from all condemnation—I'm living again. My prayer is that God will show me how to minister with the same compassion, tenderness, and acceptance that you ministered in.

Thank you for allowing me to take a minute to share with you the touch of the Lord. For your encouragement, I hope that you can sense a bit of what God did for me.

Please pay careful attention to my words: You do not have to suffer defeat any longer. There are people in the Body of Christ to whom you can turn for help. If you feel like you must talk with me about these issues, you may contact me through the offices of Impact Ministries.

Dr. Harvey R. Brown, Jr.
Impact Ministries, Inc.
304 Maxey Street, Suite E
Wilmore, Kentucky 40390

E-mail: HarveyBrown_Impact@compuserve.com

The grace of the Lord Jesus Christ be with you.

Books by Best-Selling Author
Tommy Tenney

➤ THE GOD CHASERS (National best-selling book)

There are those so hungry, so desperate for His presence, that they become consumed with finding Him. Their longing for Him moves them to do what they would otherwise never do: Chase God. But what does it really mean to chase God? Can He be "caught"? Is there an end to the thirsting of man's soul for Him? Meet Tommy Tenney—God chaser. Join him in his search for God. Follow him as he ignores the maze of religious tradition and finds himself, not chasing God, but to his utter amazement, caught by the One he had chased.
ISBN 0-7684-2016-4
Also available in Spanish
ISBN 0-7899-0642-2

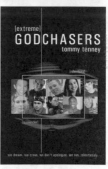

➤ EXTREME GOD CHASERS

What is an extreme God chaser? It is someone whose hunger exceeds their reach. The passionate paths of God chasers can be traced across the pages of history from Moses the young stutterer, David the dancing poet, and Paul the radical preacher, to contemporaries like A.W. Tozer, Leonard Ravenhill, and countless others who share one common bond: an insatiable hunger to know their Lord. Extreme God chasers don't apologize for their passion as they run in relentless pursuit of Christ, even though they may appear foolish in the eyes of others.
ISBN 0-7684-5001-2

➤ GOD CHASERS DAILY MEDITATION & PERSONAL JOURNAL

Does your heart yearn to have an intimate relationship with your Lord? Perhaps you long to draw closer to your heavenly Father, but you don't know how or where to start. This *Daily Meditation & Personal Journal* will help you begin a journey that will change your life. As you read and journal, you'll find your spirit running to meet Him with a desire and fervor you've never before experienced. Let your heart hunger propel you into the chase of your life…after God!
ISBN 0-7684-2040-7

➤ GOD CHASERS STUDY GUIDE

The *God Chasers Study Guide* is designed to help you develop the principles set forth in the book. You can appropriate the study guide for your own individual use or in a group setting. It is an excellent resource that will encourage and direct your personal and corporate chase of the Lord.
ISBN 0-7684-2105-5

Available at your local Christian bookstore.

6B-2:59